SIX LENSES

Other books by the same author:

The Case of the Bonsai Manager
When the Penny Drops
What the CEO Really Wants from You
A Comma in a Sentence

SIX LENSES

Vignettes of Success, Career and Relationships

R. Gopalakrishnan

RUPA

Published by
Rupa Publications India Pvt. Ltd 2016
7/16, Ansari Road, Daryaganj
New Delhi 110002

Sales Centres:

Allahabad Bengaluru Chennai
Hyderabad Jaipur Kathmandu
Kolkata Mumbai

Copyright © R. Gopalakrishnan 2016

The views and opinions expressed in this book are the author's own and the facts are as reported by him which have been verified to the extent possible, and the publishers are not in any way liable for the same.

All rights reserved.
No part of this publication may be reproduced, transmitted, or stored in a retrieval system, in any form or by any means, electronic, mechanical, photocopying, recording or otherwise, without the prior permission of the publisher.

ISBN: 978-81-291-3587-2

First impression 2016

10 9 8 7 6 5 4 3 2 1

The moral right of the author has been asserted.

Printed by Parksons Graphics Pvt. Ltd, Mumbai

This book is sold subject to the condition that it shall not, by way of trade or otherwise, be lent, resold, hired out, or otherwise circulated, without the publisher's prior consent, in any form of binding or cover other than that in which it is published.

Contents

1. Why I Wrote This Book — 1
2. What This Book Is About — 12
3. Gathering Phase of a Life — 26
4. Scattering Phase of Life — 38
5. A Theory of Career and Life — 56
6. Purpose: The First Lens — 79
7. Authenticity: The Second Lens — 94
8. Courage: The Third Lens — 113
9. Trust: The Fourth Lens — 136
10. Luck: The Fifth Lens — 156
11. Success and Fulfilment: The Sixth Lens — 174
12. My Ideas Bank — 193

Acknowledgements — 195

Index — 197

1

Why I Wrote This Book

'I saw a medieval map once. It showed the earth as a flat disc with Jerusalem in the centre. Rome was bigger than Africa, and America was not even shown, of course. The heart is that kind of map. The self is in the middle and everything is out of proportion. You draw the friends of your youth large, then it is impossible to rescale them when other more important people need to be added. Anyone who has done you wrong is shown too big, and so is any one you loved.'

—Ken Follet, *Edge of Eternity*

In February 1966, I was persuaded by friends and in my own head that in my final year at IIT, I had the credentials to win elections to the post of Vice President, Technology Students' Gymkhana. It was prestigious and high profile on the campus. Apart from a busy calendar of extra-curricular activities, the post gave one the legitimacy to talk to the very few girls on the campus. The campus was indeed conservative, so such legitimacy had huge value.

A US presidential-type election programme was to be mounted. Soap boxes and town halls in the hostels, in the play grounds and in the classes, all of these were par for the course. It lasted about two months, it was exhausting, invigorating and tiring all together. Finally on the D-day of voting in June 1966, the election result was announced. Since I had won, and by a decent margin, I was on Cloud Nine. It was an incredible feeling to represent all of IIT's 2,500 students, and to lead the Kharagpur sports contingent to the prestigious Inter IIT Sports Meet at IIT Bombay.

On a Sunday some temporary quietness and solitude descended upon me. I heard a knock on my dormitory room door. 'Hello Anil!' I said cheerfully, welcoming my long-standing friend from school classes. Anil and I had studied from Standard IV in the same school and all the way to IIT now, some twelve years in all. Anil was a brilliant student, a bit shy and reserved compared to me, and always ahead of me in the class ranks by a bit. It had been my ambition for long to top Anil, but somehow it never happened from 1954 right up until 1966. While I had been a good 'loser' to Anil in academics all these years, I was a proud 'winner' with the election results, or so I thought. Such thoughts of self-elation were flushing through my head, though unspoken and uncommunicated. I was sure that Anil had come to pump my hands and wish me all the best. But what followed was a complete shock and surprise.

Anil sat nervously at the edge of my bed, fluttered his eyes and flashed me a somewhat unfriendly stare. 'So you think you are great because you have become the Vice President of this campus. What is so great about that? Are you any the better for having won the election? There is not much difference between you and me: we are the same age, we are not too distant in academics, we have studied in the same school and now at IIT, we are dear friends and like each other. Then how come you have won elections and are being cheered by all the students on this campus? And no one even knows who I am?' he ranted with some really deep feelings of what I thought was antipathy. 'Oh my God, he is jealous! How could he do this to me?' I thought.

In an instant I had judged his behaviour to emanate from jealousy. Such an assumption allowed me to explain his behaviour completely. Quod Erat Demonstrandum. Thank God for assumptions, they help you to understand the complex world.

Soon I realised that I was dead wrong. Anil was not jealous of me, far from it. He was pained, not with me, but at his own plight. That is what he had come to express. As he narrated his life story voluntarily, he came from a home where his father was a drunkard. He described the home scene evening after evening, disruptive and tense. His mother worked extra-hard to keep the children away from the family suffering, but how much could she do? It was an emotionally disturbed environment for young Anil to grow up in.

Even now my memory of the episode shatters me. Although I cannot be blamed, I chide myself for judging Anil with wrong assumptions—especially because the wheels of fortune and fate took our lives in completely different directions. While I went on to do whatever I have done, Anil dropped out of IIT, did odd jobs, and finally had a nervous breakdown by the time he was in his 40s, and has been a resident of a mental counselling institution since then. I get to see him occasionally—I always come out feeling helpless, saddened and bewildered.

How I wish I had judged Anil correctly right in the beginning by seeing him through an alternate set of lenses.

But what are those lenses and how do you learn to view things from another perspective? It is to imagine these lenses that I set out to write this book.

What makes for success and fulfilment?

All human beings increasingly struggle with the stress of life, and particularly business executives: trying to understand and achieve what success in career and life mean; realising that the accomplishment of such success does not automatically lead to contentment and fulfilment; figuring out how to judge events and situations without judging people. The important lesson most people learn is that there is no universally accepted measure of what success is. Success depends on how the individual views his or her goals in life and how he or she thinks meaning can be found in career and life.

Understanding this reality makes success and the lenses through which to view life goals and accomplishments rather ambiguous, personal and quite wide open. And yet all the billions of people on this planet are chasing success as though it is a reality, a tangible, palpable reality!

I wrote this book to explore the nuances that lightly surround perceptions of success and fulfilment; also to appreciate the relationship of success with one's views about feeling fulfilled. The word 'vignette' in the sub-title of this book derives from a design of vine leaves, and connotes an embellishment without borders; this book is a bouquet of thoughts and ideas but with no rigid borders and framework.

Career and life books sometimes come through as offering cookie-cutter tips to avid readers who want instant, pre-packaged wisdom. They pretend to suggest action rather than inspire thinking. That is why there are several popular books on techniques, littered with the mundane and the mechanical. Frankly, if it were that easy then everybody would do it. I have not set out to author a definitive book of rules and tips about success and fulfilment.

PLU—People like us

The life stories of celebrities are highly readable and inspirational. Celebrities are written about a lot, and their stories are commented about a lot; some aspects about them also suffer exaggeration and distortion. The stories of celebrities do bear interest for the reader because celebrity stories are about people who are widely accepted to be successful. Their stories are presented like fairy tales which romanticise more than depict stark realities.

This book is based on PLU's—people like us. PLUs inspire as well as instruct readers in different ways compared to the stories of celebrities. It is comforting for ordinary people to know that PLUs, like themselves, struggle to think through dilemmas, do not know precisely what they want out of their lives and careers or struggle to live a life of fulfilment despite possessing all the trappings of success. This may perhaps be one of few such books that is based on chronicling PLUs.

PLUs are unable to recall the magical moment when 'eureka' clicked in their brain. A eureka is clicking in their brain often, but it is not recognised by them as a eureka moment and there is no thunder and lightning that blinds their mind!

These realities caused me to want to write a book from an experiential perspective—about the stories I have encountered and how they helped me think about things. I did not want to be prescriptive with pat answers and solutions to the issues of success, career and relationships. The stories involve people whom I have known, from business and society.

Why should the reader be interested in the lives of PLUs, ordinary characters? As integrated human beings, like the reader, the PLUs have three life influences: first, their genetic personality; second, their inner journey of experiences (self-awareness, mental complexity, childhood character influences); third, their outer influences (education, parents, job and friends). These three merge into one track to influence how they think and act. This integrated track defines who they are as human beings. So when you read about other people or interact with friends and work colleagues, if you wish to understand that person as an integrated human being (as you should be interested), then you need to understand that person's inner and outer life influences.

The biography and experiences of Nihal Kaviratne, Geeta and Jamshed Irani are integral to elucidating the ideas in this book.

Looking for a gap that is shaped like you

When the child born, it can be likened to a smooth pebble of a certain size and colour; both are determined by the genetics. Then as the child grows and throughout the life of the person, experiences leave an impact on the smooth pebble—chips, marks and incisions, so that each pebble develops a unique shape of its own. A France-based American writer, Ms Pamela Druckerman, expressed an imaginative view by suggesting that each person has a shape that must fit into the jigsaw of the world. 'Somewhere in the world, there is a gap shaped just like you. Once you find it, you will slide right in.'

To illustrate this point about finding a gap that is shaped just like you, I recall the story of how Leela Chitnis, India's top film star of the 1940s, found the gap shaped like her ('My Aunt Leela', *Indian Express*, October 9, 2005).

Leela was the skinny and gawky daughter of a professor; she wore thick glasses. She fell in love with an urbane gentleman who was fourteen years her senior, Dr Gajanand Chitnis, who was involved with the Marathi stage as a writer and director of plays. Dr Gajanand Chitnis was not economically successful, so the shy and self-conscious Leela started accompanying her husband to the rehearsals; she earned a bit by helping with the costumes and the sets.

Every evening she watched and observed the goings on; something must have been lodging in her brain all the time. One day, the heroine of the play failed to turn up. Leela was thrust on the stage only because she had attended the endless rehearsals. She felt hugely challenged, but she performed with a natural elan—and brilliantly. Very soon roles poured in. Then she signed for her first film.

Until 1940 Lux soap was always advertised with foreign film stars because Indians thought it poor character to model for advertisements. In 1940, when Lux sought Indian models, Leela was the first to be chosen. Soon thereafter, she became the leading Hindi film star. In her quest for a gap she could fit into, she viewed events and things differently from other people.

As Leela's story of apparent coincidences demonstrates, Leela found the gap that was shaped like her.

Differing views of the world

When we see world maps, we are used to seeing the Americas on the left side and Europe and Africa approximately in the middle. New Zealand appears in the bottom far-right corner. When I visited New Zealand, I found an interesting, almost unrecognisable version of a world map, constructed from a New Zealand perspective. New Zealand was right in the upper middle of the map. The mass of Europe, Asia and Africa spread from below upwards on the right side, like a mushroom. The Americas appeared on the left, but with the United States and Canada below Brazil. Argentina was above Brazil and was sticking upwards. They had merely turned the map upside down and placed New Zealand at the centre. The map presented a reality through a different lens (http://www.flourish.org/upsidedownmap/). The imagery of this New Zealand-centred world map makes a subtle point about what we remember of what we see.

So here is the message. We lead our lives in concentric circles. In the first circle, there is a big 'I'. The nuclear family appears, large and close. In the second circle, there appear childhood friends, school friends as well as relatives. In the third circle, we accommodate college friends, work acquaintances and relationships. In the fourth circle, there are casual friends and easy-to-forget relationships and episodes. In such a map of concentric circles, the deeply impactful people for you, whether positively or negatively, appear to be large and the others less so.

The brain stores memories of people and events differently for different people even though those people witness or experience the same event. This multiplicity is captured brilliantly in the 1950 Japanese film *Rashomon*, directed by Akira Kurosawa. A woodcutter and a priest are sitting together under a shelter, trying to stay dry under a heavy downpour of rain. A commoner joins, thus making a three-some, who discuss the brutal murder of a samurai warrior by a bandit in the forest a little while ago. There are multiple versions of what actually transpired— by the priest, the woodcutter, the bandit and the samurai's wife. The gripping plot of the film involves these characters providing alternative, self-serving and contradictory versions of the same incident.

A memoir is what the author remembers. A memoir is telling a truth as the writer sees it. One memoir writer discovered that her account of the first meeting with her ex-boyfriend was completely different from his. Such situations arise because the heart map of work colleagues and bosses are drawn differently by different people.

Learning from my own experiences and after deep thought, I can say:

a. Your 'shape' is determined by the way you view events and people in the world around you.
b. When you find and fit into the gap that has a 'shape' like you, you feel successful and fulfilled.

So I sat down to gather my thoughts into a book about how success, career and relationships are all inter-connected. I conjured up the idea of six lenses through which, according to me, you view the world. Most likely you are not conscious that that is how you view the world. Your view of these is influenced by what you see through the lenses on each eye.

There are no answers, just stories

Societies everywhere have found that ideas and life lessons are best communicated through anecdotes, parables and epics. Stories have proved durable and effective for centuries in civilizations all over the world. The revival of mythological themes in the Indian publishing industry in recent years is further evidence of the power of such storytelling, of the value of conversing with the heart rather than only with the head.

I have tried to bring together in this book several lessons that I have learnt through ideas, values and emotional energy.

Every person's experiences lead to extraordinary lessons for that person. Most of us have a deeply held view that our experiences are too commonplace to be of interest to anyone else. Furthermore, the effort involved in transforming commonplace experiences into lessons is daunting. That is why experiences and lessons perish with that person. The person's memories and lessons are wasted in the same manner that rainwater flows into the sea, not being effectively conserved, but accidentally helpful to the few whom the rainwater might serve on its way to the sea.

I rather like what an American radio producer, David Avram Isay, has tried. He founded *Storycorps*, which is an ongoing oral history project. Since 2003 his company has collected and archived more than 50,000 interviews with 100,000 participants, thus creating the largest single collection of voices ever gathered. His endeavour is based on the simple idea that everyone around you has a story that the world needs to hear. (http://itunes.com/apps/tedconferences/ted). His is an accurate assumption that every person has a heart-warming story to tell some other person, irrespective of how ordinary that person might be.

The idea of this book came to my mind out of my struggle to reconcile many aspects of work and family life—questions such as:

- How can you reconcile differing views of the same person?
- How can a person get the best out of both career and relationships?
- Are there fixed features of good character and a good life?
- Can character be consistent under all circumstances?
- How can one be inspired by others' leadership while accepting their faults?
- Is our perception of others based on whether their virtues are emphasised or their failings?
- How can one reconcile others' virtues and failings simultaneously?
- Do external events constitute a balanced and fulfilling life or an internal mind-set?

In order to resolve these struggles, I tried reading a few books of philosophy. Some of them helped a little. I think humans are born to learn, not to be taught. To illustrate this point about human beings being born to learn, not to be taught, I recall the story of B.K. Nehru, a scion of the eponymous Nehru family.

A cousin of the former Indian Prime Minister, B.K. Nehru was conversing with his London School of Economics professor Harold Laski some fifteen years after his graduation. A bit hesitatingly, Nehru told his professor that he had found little use of the professor's teachings during his practical career in the Indian Civil Service. The deep-thinking Laski responded, 'That is quite okay. I was not trying to teach you lessons in economics; I was merely teaching you how to think. And that I seem to have done very well, from what you say.'

I needed something practical. I needed somebody to chat with me rather than enlighten me. I needed a story or a conversation about how to think about the dilemma rather than a pat answer.

I needed authentic and practical examples, at least some from the life stories of real people, people like myself rather than well-known figures.

However, I am cautious about parsing success into a formula. Career and life cannot be run through formulae. That is one reason why the reader will not find a summary of the points or tips at the end of each chapter. There are no formulae, there has to be further thought and introspection by the reader.

I found that the challenge of writing up life experiences into instructive, and perhaps inspiring, stories is not faced by me alone. If only experienced people, who have developed patterns out of their life's incidents, would write their version of the dilemmas they faced, would it not be valuable? The book need not be only about rich and famous people; it must include ordinary people, the kind of people one encounters during one's career and life.

It appears that you can write your way to happiness. Scientific studies have revealed that writing about oneself and personal experiences can be beneficial to health. We all have a personal narrative that shapes our view of the world and ourselves. By writing and then editing our own stories, we can change our perception of ourselves and identify obstacles that stand in our way of enjoying well-being. So, at the very least, I stand to benefit!

I must confess a huge vulnerability. Would I be up to this task? Did I have the depth and background to explore such a subject? Maybe.

As psychologist Brene Brown has stated in her much-viewed TED talks, it is perhaps best to confront one's vulnerabilities. It could be the best way to deal with that enervating sense of vulnerability if it is standing between expressing oneself fully and keeping quiet. I decided to confront my vulnerability about whether my narrative would be interesting to the anonymous reader out there.

2

What This Book is About

'You see a green object looks green, not because it is inherently green. It looks green because the object retains all colours and reflects back green. To retain something, you should not keep it, you should give it back to others. If you want to be joyful, throw joy at others. When you have money and share with others, then you will be seen as generous. The context matters.'

—late Father Jacques de Bonhome,
Professor, St Xavier's College, Kolkata

This book is based on an obvious idea. I know it is obvious because the mark of a blindingly obvious idea is that it is usually ignored. The obvious idea is that we judge people and events through assumptions which we have adopted, consciously or unconsciously. So the key message of this book is that we lead our lives under the impression that there is a reality, but, in fact, there is only our perception of a reality. Our feeling of success and fulfilment are influenced by our perceptions, and perceptions are influenced by the lenses through which we see the world. By rotating the lenses through which we view the world, we change our perceptions; and by changing our perceptions, we can reconsider what success and fulfilment mean to us. This key message is the substance of the book.

There is a film sequence that brings out clearly how widely different the perception can be about what constitutes life's accomplishments. In the film *Deewaar,* there is a dialogue between two long-lost brothers (Amitabh Bachchan and Shashi Kapoor), separated in their childhood. They reconnected many years later and discovered their identities. The powerful and arrogant brother boasted about his accomplishments and possessions, 'I have lots of money, a big house, pomp and power. What have you got?' The modest brother dramatically responded, 'I have with me our dear mother whose blessings are my treasure.' The brothers were viewing their accomplishments through very different lenses.

A person who is beautiful tends to judge the world in terms of attention and attraction. A hugely wealthy person may judge other people through their display of wealth. The way you measure yourself is usually how you measure others, and how you assume others measure you. That is why we have such different measures of what constitutes success and fulfilment.

Career, work and relationships

Work accounts for a huge proportion of our lives. Work occupies about a third of our physical life because work occupies about a third of any day. But work affects almost all of our emotional and psychological life. Our professional accomplishments, the position we reach and the success that we achieve seem to define who we are, how others perceive us, and all the trappings that come with work. An apparently small issue at work, like a stressed relationship with a boss or colleague can spill over into personal or domestic life in a disproportionate way. Why do we work? To get influence. There is an intimate but causal connection between work and influence.

The word 'relationships' is used in a broad sense: partner,

spouse, children, siblings, school cohorts, work colleagues and friends. There is a deep and causal link between relationships and the enjoyment of life. Nobody who has friends fails to enjoy life. Conversely, a person with few friends has a higher chance of suffering through his or her life. Poor relationships destroy mental peace and human harmony. People rarely succeed unless they have fun in what they are doing.

A great source of urban tension is the work–relationships balance. Paying enough attention and giving enough time to both is not easy. We tend to view work and family as being opposed, and that there is a polarisation between work and family; you can have one or the other, but not both. According to this perception, there is a constant search for compromise. However this is not true.

As we go through our lives, we experience many events and episodes. For instance, a person may give up opportunities for his or her professional advancement in order to take care of parents. Viewed through the lens of work, the person's decision does not appear impressive. But viewed through the lens of purpose and family, the person might well appear to be responsible and sensitive. Both are valid views, depending on the lenses through which the event is viewed.

Later in this book, Nihal Kaviratne's story is narrated about how and why he gave up a chance to study at Harvard. He did so to ensure he did not lose his love in life. Nihal's story exemplifies the point that such choices are not compromises or accommodations. Such choices maximise that person's sense of self-worth.

The quest for success and fulfilment

As managers and human beings, our sense of fulfilment is shaped by our search for meaning through our work experiences, dilemmas, conflicts, successes and failures. The quest for fulfilment is what makes us loyal to causes, bosses or to companies. The quest for fulfilment makes us behave with a cynical or suspicious temperament. The quest for fulfilment makes us slaves to either wealth or public benefaction. The quest for fulfilment can make us happy, contented people or possibly angry, frustrated individuals.

Contrary to feelings of victimisation when we are faced with difficulties, we are not victims of our circumstances—we make choices. We do not compromise our life, we decide our life and its course. When we think of our decision as a compromise, there is always the lingering feeling that we have sacrificed something unhappily. If you give up something happily, then you do not feel a compromise has been made; you feel you have made a choice. In this manner we instinctively shape our attitudes and live our lives to weave them into a design that defines who we are, what we want to do in our lives and what makes us happy.

Read about this real life incident in which a choice was made by a job-seeking candidate.

The job candidate who arrived late

Company Director R.V. Raghavan (*What Professional Managers Can Learn from Family Businesses,* TMTC Journal of Management, January 2012) narrated this incident which occurred during a whole day of interviews he did while seeking a candidate to join his company. I have reproduced it with the permission of the author and TMTC:

> 'Ensconced in my hotel room, I was feeling increasingly incensed that my 10 am appointment had not turned up even though the clock was close to striking eleven. I had set aside the day for meeting a number of candidates for a senior opening, and the day had not commenced well. Just as my thoughts were turning to the next appointment, the bell rang rather loudly and insistently. Lo behold, this turned out to be the first candidate.

'He was a trifle breathless, perspiring, with clothes that laid no pretence to crease. He barged in even before the customary civilities had been completed, collapsed on the sofa, took out a handkerchief to wipe his palms and forehead and proceeded to heave a rather large briefcase on to the coffee table. In what rapidly raised my consternation, he opened the briefcase, took out a gift-wrapped box and offered it to me with great alacrity. Bristling with impatience and embarrassment, I turned sharply towards him and asked him what this was for.

'I have been married for over fifteen years' he explained 'and after all these years, we have been blessed with a baby boy this morning. I am coming straight from the nursing home, and as you are the first person I am meeting, I would like you to share in my joy'.

'That incident, more than any other I can recall, brought home to me rather starkly how very conditioned, righteous and self-assured professional managers can be in their attitudes and approach: and how essential it was not to jump to conclusions when confronted with situations that are not as structured and seemingly logical as their professional training and exposure might have led them to expect. That degree of openness, bereft of presumptions or pre-conceived notions is an essential mind set to dispassionately examining and determining what professional managers can usefully learn from family-managed businesses.'

So how would a psychologist have analysed this? Let me try.

Situation: The director was on a rushed trip to hire a suitable candidate for his company or department.

His Perception: This candidate does not care about the job I might be able to offer because he cannot even arrive on time. How on earth could he be a potential candidate to join my firm?

His Need: To find a technically competent and disciplined candidate for his firm or department.

Thus: He is furious and takes the decision not to consider that late-comer of a candidate.

Afterwards the situation and analysis looked like this.

Situation: The director was on a rushed trip to hire a suitable candidate for the firm or his department.

His Perception: This candidate is a really good human being. He did what was right for his family, and it is so natural an instinct to be with his wife when she was ready to deliver a long-awaited baby. He is a caring person.

His Need: To recruit a good human being who is also technically competent.

Thus: Well, let me give him a chance to show his experience and knowledge. I should be understanding.

This simple but true story is the day to day story for every person: you just change the context, view the same facts through different lenses, and you judge things quite differently.

An experiment was conducted in an American university through which an actor who acted the role of an academic managed to persuade distinguished academics that he too was a brilliant academic!

The expert Dr Myron Fox

An experiment was conducted at the University Of Southern California School Of Medicine in 1970 in which two speakers gave lectures to a classroom of MDs and PhDs (psychiatrists and psychologists) on an irrelevant topic. The topic, 'Mathematical Game Theory as Applied to Physician Education', was chosen to eliminate the factor that the students being lectured may know anything about the actual subject. Students were divided into two separate classrooms; one classroom would be lectured by an actual scientist and the other by an actor who was given the identity of Dr Myron L. Fox, a graduate of Albert Einstein College of Medicine.

In the first half of the study the actor was instructed to teach his material in a more staccato and inexpressive voice. This lecture was then compared to the control lecture by the scientist. After the lectures, the students were tested on the information they had learned and the students who attended the lecture taught by the scientist learned more about the material, and performed better on the examination.

However, when both 'Dr Myron L. Fox' and the scientist presented their material in an engaging, expressive, and enthusiastic manner, the students rated Dr Fox just as highly as the genuine professor. This lack of correlation between content-coverage and ratings under conditions of high expressiveness became known as the Dr Fox Effect.

The experimenters created a meaningless lecture on 'Mathematical Game Theory as Applied to Physician Education,' and coached the actor to deliver it 'with an excessive use of double talk, neologisms, non sequiturs, and contradictory statements.' At the same time, the researchers encouraged the actor to adopt a lively demeanor, convey warmth toward his audience, and intersperse his nonsensical comments with humor... The actor fooled not just one, but three separate audiences of professional and graduate students. Despite the emptiness of his lecture, fifty-five psychiatrists, psychologists, educators, graduate students and other professionals produced evaluations of Dr Fox that were overwhelmingly positive...The disturbing feature of the Dr Fox study, as the experimenters noted, is that Fox's nonverbal behaviors so completely masked a meaningless, jargon-filled, and confused presentation.

A subsequent research study found that prestige of research could even be increased by confounding writing style, with research competency being positively correlated to reading difficulty. In the world of management, possibly in every area of human knowledge, we do encounter situations where bombast passes off as expertise, don't we?

This Fox experiment clearly brings out how a total non-expert managed to convey an impression to experts that he himself was an expert! Perception can actually be modified to alter what the reality is—by turning the lenses through which a situation is viewed.

It is incredible but true that normal, intelligent people can be psyched to believe untrue things. Here is the well-known case of how perfectly sensible and educated people were made to believe completely untrue things by placing them in a particular context.

Philip Zimbardo alive

Religion and social etiquette teach us that most people are basically good, but that some become less good or actually bad. In other words, the majority are good people, but some become bad people. Former Stanford professor, Philip Zimbardo, said recently the opposite: we all (emphasis all) can be evil! (http://www.nytimes.com/2015/philip-zimbardo). What made Zimbardo say that? It was his experiment fifty years ago.

In 1971, academic Zimbardo conducted an experiment at Stanford University. A part of the basement of the psychology department was converted into a mock prison with bars, cells et al. An advertisement for student volunteers elicited a generous response and twenty-one were selected. Some were 'appointed' as guards while some others were prisoners. Zimbardo himself became the prison superintendent. The objective of the exercise was to determine why prisons are such nasty places. It could be because nasty people go to prison or prisons are so nasty that good people become nasty.

Soon the 'guards' unleashed a terror regime to control the prisoners. Even though the students were all normal, nice, pacifist people, the intensity and speed of their conversion to nasty guards took everyone by surprise. It became so nasty that the experiment had to be stopped ahead of planned time.

Many years later, when interviewed, one of the guards, David Eshleman (now running a home loan company in California) claimed that he did not turn nasty, he was merely trying to please the superintendent, Zimbardo. Another guard, John Mark, recalled the event as nothing bad happened, it was just a boring experiment. Zimbardo insists that 'evil environments turn most people, not necessarily all, to behave in an evil way.' He quotes Germany's Auschwitz and I remember Indian Partition.

Whatever the academics aver out of this experiment, the fact is that by a turn of the lenses, the so-called reality can be changed into a different perception.

What you see is not what there is

In 1962 I began to attend the physics classes of Father Jacques de Bonhome, a Belgian Jesuit who taught physics at St Xavier's College Kolkata. He had a physics degree from a European university and there was something distinctive about his understanding of young students as well as the art of teaching. I remember him as a tall, wiry figure with an aquiline nose and high cheek bones on his rather thin face; De Bonhome looked serious and austere, although that veneer hid a caring and warm teacher.

Father de Bonhome was the first one who sprinkled onto my curious, young mind the mysterious message, 'what you see is not what there is'!

Father de Bonhome was teaching optics, not philosophy. What did he mean by saying 'what you see is not what there is'? 'You see colours through your eyes. Remember the basic rainbow colours of violet, indigo, blue, green, yellow, orange and red. When all of these colours combine, you get white,' he would say with the mastery of simplifying complex science. 'When white light falls on any object, the object, based on its own nature, selectively retains some colours and reflects back some others. So when you see a green shirt, it does not mean that the shirt is actually green. It merely means that the shirt has absorbed all colours other than green and throws back the green colour to you as the observer,' de Bonhome would state with his lilting Belgian French accent. 'So the green shirt is not green, it looks green because green is what it returns to you.'

And then he would add with the tone of Jesuit renunciation, 'You see, to retain something, you should not keep it, you should give to back others. If you want to be joyful, throw joy at others. When you have money, give it to others, then only will you look generous. The context matters.'

With his flair for mysterious-sounding statements, Father de Bonhome would teach us about stroboscopic effects. My reader need not be put off by this high-sounding term. It is the simple reason why, for example, in a movie reel, the cart-wheel appears to move backwards when the cart is moving forwards. Our eyes flicker at 60 CPS (cycles per second). Any moving object that is bathed in light which is flickering at 60 CPS will appear to be stationary to the human eye. So fluorescent tube lights are programmed to flicker at 60 CPS, so also are our television screens.

Thus Father de Bonhome delivered two messages: first, that the context influences our perception of the nature of objects placed into that context; second, that the frequency of light influences our perception. So there is no reality, there is only perception. Gosh, is there no reality according to physics?

After graduating in 1967 when I underwent the standard medical tests before being appointed as a computer trainee in Hindustan Lever, Medical Officer Dr Ramnik Parekh presented me some circles with coloured dots inside. After asking me to identify the numbers coloured within, he said with a tone of discovery, 'Oh, you are partially colour-blind!' I was crestfallen and thought that my budding career was about to be derailed by this natty looking doctor in half-sleeves. 'No, it will not affect your career unless you try to become an airline pilot or artist,' he announced cheerfully and I went on to join Hindustan Lever.

Years later, I read what colour vision scientists had to say about my long-standing question, is it possible that what many see as red colour is seen as blue by some others? Jay Neitz, University of Washington, and Joseph Carroll, Medical College of Wisconsin, both say that people do not all see colours in the same way. There are colour-sensitive cones in our brains and these can make one person see blood as red, while another sees blood as blue. I always thought that blood had to be red, and that was a reality! Not true.

Animals and insects perceive the same reality differently from us humans. Unlike humans who have simple eyes, insects have compound eyes. Insects have thousands of hexagonal lenses through which signals reach their brains. That is why a fly sees your fly-swatter device moving towards it as a leisurely pace, thus helping the insect to avoid getting swatted, whereas you have moved the swatter at a furious pace! (*The Economist*, July 25, 2015).

What you taste is not the taste it is

We tend to think of food preferences as largely to do with taste, though it is a much more complex phenomenon called flavour. Our tongue has only five taste receptors: sweet, sour, bitter and salt are the traditionally known taste receptors. Only in recent years have we learnt about a fifth taste receptor, umami (literally 'yummy') which makes certain foods savoury tasty.

However it appears that it is not just these five receptors that account for what we think as taste of food. Perception is influenced, in addition, by over four hundred smell receptors. These smell receptors work in distinctive combinations. For example if you take in a sharp breath, hold your breath and then eat a banana, you will find the banana to be a somewhat flavourless item. But if you breathe out while eating the banana, it tastes like a banana. Try this and see how the context can change the perception of how a banana tastes.

What is happening is that the brain reconstructs what our senses are reading and we assume that what we sense is real. But it is not anything real, it is merely the brain at work.

The brain constructs our reality

As early as 1868, Thomas Huxley had said that there is a definite connection between the brain activity and our conscious experiences. I listened to Donald Hoffman, cognitive scientist, speak in June 2015 at TED (http://itunes.com/apps/tedconferences/ted) about whether we experience the world as it really is. His speech left my unprepared mind a bit confused because his well-presented arguments challenged my long-standing assumptions. What Hoffman states is difficult to understand at first, 'Space and time are like the computer interface, and objects are like the icons on the screen. There is no reality to space, time and objects.' According to Hoffman, 'space, time and objects, which we think as being reality, are, believe it or not, reconstructions by our brains of what we see based on our assumptions.'

The importance of assumptions bears repetition. When everybody perceived the reality of the world as being flat, the view that the world is round just would not register; likewise for the assumption that the sun rotates around the earth, not the other way around. With regard to evolution, we have grown up with the age-old assumption that the ability to see reality accurately confers an evolutionary advantage through, for example, early detection of predators. The ability to see reality clearly may be nothing more than possessing a firm set of assumptions, which, incidentally, may be wrong! Experiments have shown that those who see accurately (firmer assumptions) may in fact have poorer survival chances than those who see inaccurately!

Based on experimentation in the recent decades, Donald Hoffman says that there may be no objective reality around us; our mind reconstructs reality (note it does not construct, but reconstructs) for us based on the assumptions we have unconsciously made.

Phew, what lessons? From optics to life. I cannot forget Father Jacques de Bonhome, partly for giving me the love of physics, but also for putting the profound thought that there may be no reality into my plastic mind. It all depends on what your eyes see and how your brain processes the sight.

The colour that I see as reality may not be a reality. The moving object that I see may not be moving in the way that I perceive. My brain is reconstructing what I see on the basis of my assumptions about life and things. There is no reality, there are only perceptions created through the human eyes and the human brain!

We see each other as the person we see in flesh and distinct—father, mother, teacher, friend, colleague. Physicists will tell you that we are comprised mostly of empty space—molecules, atoms, electrons, quarks and so on. Biologists will tell you that we are what the micro-bacteria do in our gut. I suppose that is why any of us fits into a small urn when we are done and cremated.

But this is when my brain button ticks. Is this not what ancient Indian philosophers stated centuries ago? But like every one of my readers, I reckon that I try to understand the sayings of my ancestors through the academics of modern neuroscience.

The six lenses idea

If there is no reality in the way we tend to think of reality, then it can be a most bewildering world to live in. Indeed it is. If the world is bewildering (and complex), it is difficult to make sense and that in itself can lead to a great deal of stress. That is why man needs a mental model, which can help to simplify the world and help to lead a happy life with sanity.

In chapter 5, I describe how I arrived at a model that can help our brain to understand why we see things the way we do, why others see the same thing differently, and how we can, if we wish, change the way we see things.

Imagine that you are viewing people and events through an optician's eye-testing frame. There is a left eye and a right eye. The left eye represents the world of work, perspectives from the professional arena of employment and influence. The right eye represents the arena of the family, relationships and enjoyment.

On the support frame of the optician, there are lenses that can be rotated to improve vision during testing. The rotation of each lens changes the clarity and the view. There are zillions of perspectives that the viewer can get. He or she has to select the view that best suits him or her. Our perception of events in life is a bit like these two eyes, watching and judging things through the lenses on each eye. There are six lenses that shape our perception of the leadership challenges encountered in work and family: purpose, authenticity, courage, trust, luck and fulfilment.

More of these and many anecdotes in the rest of the book…

The book has a chapter that corresponds to each of the six lenses I mentioned. Each chapter leads in with the stories of real persons, with the facts. Anyway, there's nothing like the 'full facts'; nobody but nobody knows the 'full facts'. Life is all about getting on with an appreciation of as many facts as possible.

3

Gathering Phase of a Life

'A man's past keeps growing even when his future has come to a standstill.'

—Aravind Adiga, *Last Man in Tower*

In the eponymous novel by Aravind Adiga, Masterji Yogesh Murthy is one of the residents of Vishram Cooperative Housing Society at Vakola, Mumbai. He had been a science schoolteacher for thirty-three years. His neighbours respect him for his knowledge and age, but perceive him as a quaint product of the past. Masterji is a widower who, unfortunately, has also lost his daughter. Fellow residents living in the building see Masterji as an old man, a man whose past keeps growing when his future has come to a standstill. But Masterji does not think of himself in the same way. He reckons he has much to do still and that is Masterji's inner view about his life and experiences. Throughout the novel, Masterji's actions are guided by his assumptions about himself, while others find him very difficult to understand because of their assumptions about him.

With many people, the first part of life is spent in what I call the 'gathering phase' while the second part is spent in the 'scattering phase.' In the gathering phase, the individual is focused on improving financial status, power, wealth and things that are acquisitive in nature. In the second part of career and life, a person goes through a scattering phase when the person seeks and wants to share experiences, time and even wealth with others; in this way the individual seeks meaning to life.

The story of Nihal Kaviratne that follows in this chapter demonstrates these very well. His story is, in fact, presented as the gathering phase, followed by the scattering phase.

Everyone can view his or her life from inside as the protagonist to whom things are happening, or from the outside as an observer who watches things that are happening. In the first view, you are the actor. In the second view, you are the audience. The British philosopher, Jonathan Glover, said that if we really want to understand ourselves, we need to achieve a sort of intellectual binocularity, which is an ability to view ourselves through two eyes: in any situation we are both the subject and the object.

Life stories help to achieve this intellectual binocularity because the narrator tells a story by viewing himself as a subject with free choices, and also an object, which happens to be what it is. The following life story exemplifies the point, but, more importantly, it tells the story of an ordinary person.

Nihal Kaviratne was born from a Sri Lankan father and an Indian Catholic mother. He was raised with Western influences; early on, he became a vegetarian with such a soft heart that he revolted against all forms of unfairness and injustice. He gave up a chance to study at Harvard because he so feared that he might lose his precious girlfriend, whom he courted, married and stayed married to for the rest of his life. He retired from a senior executive position after a forty-year stint at Unilever. He had earned and saved well during his career. His family consisted of his wife and daughter, Shyama and Mallika, and the loyal Smita, treated like a family member, but not related by blood—how she came to be a virtual family member is an important part of the narrative. Looking to do something useful after retirement, the narrative tells the reader how he chanced upon the dire condition of cancer-affected children who don't have a clean and safe home from where to get treated for cancer. He went on to set up an institution called St Jude. Whereas Unilever was his first preoccupation for forty years, it is now St Jude, which defines who he is, what his life means to him and how immensely fulfilling it is for him.

It may appear that the details of his life story tell the reader little. But it is a whole narrative, and I expect that different readers will consider different details to be irrelevant. But here is the full story from the subject, looking back at his life as though he were a spectator.

To repeat what was said in the last chapter, we are integrated human beings with genetic influences, inner influences and outer influences. You will see all of these in active inter-play in this narrative.

Nihal Kaviratne's childhood

Nihal Kaviratne CBE, 71, is a portly man with twinkling eyes. He has the mannerism of periodically stroking his head as though he were settling his hair, which is largely non-existent. He comes through as a man of apparently easy manner, but is, in reality, a man of great determination. I should know because he had been my contemporary in Hindustan Lever and our careers and families tracked together for many years. He has been immensely successful in his professional career and his personal life. He certainly feels complete. He is not rich or famous, but he has been successful, has provided well for his family and rightly feels that he has accomplished much with his life. Importantly, his spirit and view are in concurrence that that there is more to be achieved—like Masterji.

I recorded our conversation and am keeping to the conversational style in this chapter.

RG: *Nihal, I would request you to just say a few words about your background and your early life.*

NK: Like it happens with most of us, the early influences get stored on to a hard disc, which then gets drawn on as one gets older and as beliefs and attitudes begin to harden. My father was Sri Lankan Sinhalese, and came from an old family of agricultural traders. My great grandfather made a lot of money and built Kaviratne Place, which is still a fine address in Colombo.

My great grandfather was not happy with my grandfather, who liked the good life. He loved cigars, he loved his drink and he was not very good at the family business. In fact, he lost some of the business that my great grandfather had developed. Finally, Kaviratne Place had to be torn down and the proceeds split among various cousins. The family graveyard still exists and the place is still called Kaviratne Place.

My father started working in the Galle Face Hotel in Colombo and took an interest in two things, aeronautics and archaeology. He became an aeronautical engineer, but, on the side, also an amateur archaeologist. He joined a French expedition which was engaged in excavating in the ruins of Kandahar for civilizations as old as Mohenjo-daro and Harappa. The closest aircraft factory was quite far away, the HAL factory in Bangalore. So, in 1942, he worked his way to Bangalore, found a job in HAL and he continued his archaeological interest in Kandahar with the French expedition. I remember he used to bring my mother some wonderful stuff, like bracelets, from the ruins there (things that they were allowed to take away officially). Anyway, this was 1942 and he was in pre-Independence Bangalore.

My mother's father was a doctor in Rangoon in Burma, and his brother was a pharmacist. Together they had a very nice setup in Rangoon. They made decent money and had a nice network of patients. My mother's father was an Anglophile, and he made sure my mother and her sisters were taught Western classical music. He brought them up in a western sort of way in what was then British Burma. He had an abiding faith that the British would never allow the Japanese to enter and take Burma, so the family stayed on despite the fact that everyone else was leaving the country. When the Japanese did arrive, the family took the last boat out from Rangoon and landed in Calcutta. An interesting aside is that one of the co-passengers on the boat was a Mr Mentzelopoulos. Many years later I met his daughter, Ms Corinne Mentzelopoulos, of the French winemaker Chateau Margaux with whom I am now connected with to build the image of Chateau Margaux in India.

My mother's family worked their way down from Calcutta to Bangalore. My maternal grandfather was a broken man because his wife, that's my grandmother, died of cancer. It tore him that even as a doctor he could do nothing about it. In Bangalore he started a modest business, again as a medical practitioner. He died three years later at the relatively young age of fifty-three. I think I was three years old at the time of his death.

Thus it was that my parents met in Bangalore. I was born in Bangalore out of the love marriage of Hubert Sumarasinghe Kaviratne and Madeline Lazarus. The early years were wonderful, full of birthday parties for my sister and I who were two years apart. We were brought up with values that were very much western.

In religious terms, I had an unusual cocktail of influences. My great grandmother was a Brahmin and a devout Hindu. My grandfather on my mother's side had converted to Catholicism. My mother was a staunch Catholic. I was baptised and so was my sister. My father's entire family were Buddhists. Many years later, my wife, Shyama, and I went to Sri Lanka on our honeymoon.

My uncle, who was the secretary of the Mahabodhi Society there, made sure that we got married according to Buddhist rites. So this melange of three religions has always been a part of me. The way of life these three religions have embedded in them have had an impact on me that has been long-lasting.

RG: *How has this melange of religions influenced your thinking?*

NK: It stimulated my curiosity and, most recently, I started taking interest in two other monotheistic religions, Islam and Judaism. They continue to be so and I wonder why they cannot find some ecumenical common ground.

But something else also happened. You know that I am a vegetarian. The first influence is the Brahmin influence of my great grandmother. She used to tell me that my father was an evil man because he was trying to feed me animal protein to make me strong and to grow. I eschewed meat because of my great grandmother and her influence. Nevertheless, I would eat some meats if they were very heavily disguised in flavour (like sausages) despite my great grandmother.

The second influence was an episode. At the age of nine, I received an airgun as a present and I used to shoot at targets. One day in the bedroom of our house, there was a sparrow sitting close to the ceiling and I took a pot-shot at it. I wounded it and it fell. I nursed it for several days despite my father telling me that it was dead. That was probably one of the turning points in my life. It's a small thing, but from that day I've never been able to countenance physical pain and the death of any living creature. I can't even swat a mosquito.

To this day, those vegetarian roots have survived, much to the amusement of many people, who look at my size and my western upbringing and just cannot understand why I am vegetarian. But it went much beyond the physical because I started seeing people and aspects through a different lens.

RG: *I am interested that you use the word 'lens' because my thesis for this book is that life is all about the lens through which you view your experiences.*

NK: I agree with your thesis—life is indeed about lenses. That is why the same episode can have different effects on different people. It was around the time I turned vegetarian that this care for people who were in some way weaker than myself took root, not necessarily underprivileged or poor people but those weaker than me in some way. My heart always went out to them. I will never forget the day my sister and I were in a rickshaw coming back from school. We saw a ragged man on the street. We stopped and asked him what he was looking for. He had dropped four *annas*, which was the currency in those days. He was distraught and searching furiously for those four *annas*. My sister and I went home to my parents, who were not at home. An English lady friend of my mother was visiting. We begged her for four *annas* and took the coins and rushed back to the place where this man was. We couldn't find him. I can never forget this episode because what that man was looking for was all of just four *annas*. I have since then always had this huge desire to help bring equality in terms of strength to those who are in some need, especially those who are worse off than me.

My parents' marriage broke up. As a result, during the traumatic years leading up to the split, I went off to boarding school for three years. There are two people in my life who taught me virtually all that I know. One was my mother, who taught me how to wire an electric plug and at least half of everything else that I know. The other half was taught to me later by my boss and friend, Rajesh Bahadur, but more about him later.

The three years at boarding school helped me gain independence from my mother, to whom I was very, very attached. Later on, she got custody of my sister and me. We came to live in Mumbai. My father married a German lady and went away to Germany. I have two stepsisters from my father's second marriage (they now live in Spain and Portugal). My mother married a Parsi gentleman surnamed Vicaji, who was the first cousin of Thelly Vicaji, also known as Mrs JRD Tata.

During those years another thing happened. My mother and my stepfather lived larger than real life and they were always spending more than they were earning. So they were always in debt. As a result there were continuing moments of cash crisis. Not that it ever meant that they denied me anything, but there was always the tension and anxiety of a cash crunch because they were spending more than they were earning.

RG: *So this observation by a growing person provided yet another lens through which you viewed earning, spending and money?*

NK: Absolutely. One of the things that got deeply embedded in me at that time was that I was never going to be in debt and that I would do everything I could to save; and save not just for myself but to make sure that everyone who was dependent on me was safe. None of my family should ever want for anything. I would save more of what I earned than I would spend. And that also has always been a strong driving force for me from those years. I then went on to The Cathedral & John Connon School in Bombay, as had my stepfather and, later, my daughter.

Reaching for high-hanging fruit

Through all of this narrative, Nihal displayed a sense of self-control. He seemed to be able to postpone gratification of things he craved for, like money and family love. I was curious to know more, 'Is it a characteristic of yours to postpone indulgence? Did something influence you to learn things like 'earn now and think of spending it later'?'

NK: Yes, you are right. I developed a huge habit of delaying gratification. It is a belief I developed about twenty years ago and it spread beyond money into other areas as well. It spread into, for example, looking for the hard things to do, eschewing the low-hanging fruit. I'm not much for low-hanging fruit; I really do believe it is for the goats. I like stretching my head out like the giraffe for the high-hanging fruit.

This manifests itself in what some people think of as strange habits. For instance, in the office when I would review the inbox of papers or, today, the email inbox, I never succumb to the temptation of dealing with the easy ones first. I always seek out the most difficult ones and try and go for those. Delaying gratification is an extension of this habit. As a result, I have found myself taking on the most risky tasks, those that don't have a high probability of success. Consequently, I have many failures to my name. But I can't find myself picking off low-hanging fruit; it just doesn't do anything to me. Things that take longer to fructify are what I like.

At Cathedral, as most of us were then, I had a lot of girlfriends. After school I wanted to go to St Xavier's because that was where all the fun was reported to be. My stepfather advised me to seek the counsel of Tata Sons director Mr R.D. Choksi. He steered me to Elphinstone College and, therefore, it was to Elphinstone College that I went. I had a wonderful four years there. If I were to pick the five best periods of my life, the years at Elphinstone would be among them. I was in great form there. I became the chairman of the students' union. I got involved in all kinds of activities, developed my amateur dramatics interests (I joined Alyque Padamsee's theatre group) and also took up debating. Mr Choksi's steering me to Elphinstone had several unintended consequences—like my meeting Shyama, staying on in India, and so on—that have worked to my benefit.

While in college I used to do things which were the opposite of what others did, to delay gratification and go for the high-hanging fruit. If, for example, I had to answer four questions in an exam paper, I would answer thoroughly the one that really interested me, maybe write 36 pages on just that one question, with huge depth and intensity. The others were not answered. The result was that I would just about pass. In fact, the examiner would, on the one hand, feel so sorry at me not completing the exam paper, but, on the other hand, be very impressed with my strange character. Because I did that one question with such enormous depth, they would pass me. I ended up getting a second class in BA Economics, not a poor result in Bombay University at the time.

Secure my love or risk it

I met Shyama in college and fell deeply in love with her. She came from a completely different family background. Her mother was from a traditional Gujarati Ahmedabad family. Shyama had to actually bathe before going to see her grandmother. They were a strict Vaishnav family. Her father, a senior executive in a Swiss insurance company, came from a family of Surti Nagar Brahmins, her grandfather was an Indian Civil Services officer and served as prime minister in various princely states.

Anyway, we met and it took some time for me to woo her, which I did. We were both sixteen, just out of school and in the first year at university (this was 1961). We developed a close relationship within six months of meeting and I came to know her family well. At the end of the four years, I had a choice. I got a scholarship to go to Harvard University, which was very rare in those days. This was partly because of my extracurricular activities, which also brought me into contact with USIS at that stage. USIS sponsored me and I got a scholarship.

But I had to exercise a choice: marry Shyama and stay on in India, or go off to the United States. I knew if I went to the USA, and Shyama went her own way, that would be the end of that relationship. I didn't want that. So I stayed on and explored choices for employment, doing some temporary jobs. Initially I worked as a part-time English tutor at Elphinstone College, earning a couple of hundred rupees. I couldn't afford not to earn because my parents were not supporting me, though I was living at home. To earn I joined Avery. They offered me a good job and I was earning about Rs 1,300 a month, most of it was as commission.

In terms of career, I could have applied for the Indian Administrative Service, the Tata Administrative Service or to Hindustan Lever. I chose Hindustan Lever. I went through a series of interviews and they finally offered me a job. So I joined them in February 1966 at Rs 750 a month. My salary had been reduced but there was the prestige and my long-term future was secured. Shyama, meanwhile, had started working for Bank of Baroda.

We really struggled in the early years. I was posted in Madras and we got married a year later, in 1967. We were both twenty-three and our marriage has lasted all these years. I stayed with Unilever and I retired, in fact, in December 2005: so February 1966 to December 2005, just short of forty years. A very complete life, I must say. Our parents gave us nothing—other than two liabilities. Each side insisted that we take one family domestic help of theirs. A *bai* came from Shyama's side and a cook came from my mother's side. We had to pay these two people in addition to fending for ourselves. Of whatever we earned, we saved some, and we kept saving, saving, saving, saving.

Sometime later we had Mallika. Since Shyama was also working, we needed someone to look after the child. Although at that time we were in Bombay, and both sets of grandparents were there, we wanted to be on our own. We came across a Maharashtrian lady who had suffered some traumatic experiences and was looking for a home. That is how Smita, from Khed in the interiors of Maharashtra, came to live with us.

Smita has become a part of our home, part of our family.

She has her own room in our house. She eats with us. She has been with us everywhere we've travelled in the world. She is taken care of for life and she is now looking after my daughter's children. She has been with my daughter throughout. Even when Mallika went away to Edinburgh University, we kept a home for Smita close to her. So Smita has always looked after Mallika, and is now looking after her children. She speaks English and likes the opera. She is now a British national and she is a member of our family and my wife regards her as her sister. Smita is a wonderful human being.

Nihal spent almost forty years in Unilever, building a career and with all the trappings of a career—successes and failures, satisfactions and disappointments, arguments and harmony, ambiguity and clarity, being sure and being unsure. His career took him to various postings within India, and later, to Indonesia, the United Kingdom, Argentina, to Indonesia for a second time, and finally to Singapore.

4

Scattering Phase of Life

'I was going to take all that I had learnt at Unilever into building an organisation called St Jude, which would have the same cutting-edge quality that I had been taught. I put all I knew into St Jude, whether it was designing standard operating procedures, attention to quality or safety management. Every single thing that I learnt I put there, which is why it runs like clockwork even when I am not there. The recipe that I formulated at Unilever Indonesia was, incidentally, used by an author friend as a title for his book, Think Big, Start Small, Move Fast. I put that into St Jude as well...'

—Nihal Kaviratne

For most of us, life is no fairy tale out of a storybook. We are given the impression that it was so for Roger Federer and Yehudi Menuhin who seemed to know from the time they emerged from the womb that their life would be about tennis and music! So much for your gullibility if you believe these stories.

How did a PLU like Nihal Kaviratne find purpose in his life? How did he find such a strong purpose that could be all-consuming to him? So deep that he could derive immense fulfillment out of achieving that purpose.

Nihal stared right out of the balcony window. 'My wife and I had strong influences from both sides, from Shyama's family and from mine: an abiding interest in the welfare of underprivileged children. It started with my mother's deep-rooted passion for St Jude and Catholic orphanages. St Jude was the saint of lost and desperate causes and my mother had immense faith in him. Her faith was severely tested when my only sister died in an accident in Paris in 1974.

'The incident strengthened my mother's belief in St Jude; she survived the death of her child because of that faith. It then led her to take a strong interest in several Catholic orphanages like St Catherine's Home and St Anthony's in Bombay. On Shyama's side of the family, her grandmother, her mother and her aunts started an institution called Bal Anand in their huge home at Malabar Hill. Their objective was to look after children who went to municipal schools in the afternoons. The kids went to school during the day and, in the afternoon, instead of roaming about in the streets as vagrants they would come to Bal Anand for extracurricular activities like art-based therapy and crafts. Bal Anand still exists and runs not far from where it started.

'When Shyama and I got married, we started doing quite a lot of this ourselves. We used to regularly bring home children from orphanages, look after them and feed them. Once upon returning home, I went to the kitchen of our company flat to have a bite before going to bed. I heard some strange noises coming from the guestroom. I opened the door and saw some twenty kids fast asleep on the floor. I recall asking Shyama, 'Do you realise that the guestroom is full of kids on the floor?' She explained that they were street children with no place to stay. I said that I could get in trouble with the company for this, but she insisted that they did not have a place to stay and that they would go away during the day.

RG: *Weren't you bothered about security because, as with all big* *cities, Bombay was not exactly a safe place?'*

NK: Yes, exactly, but we traded that off and took the risk. Just as we did with a lot of the children we used to bring home, we used to go to the orphanages and work with them there as well.

Nihal's view was shaped by his mother's interest in Catholic organisations and, in Shyama's case, by her family's Bal Anand institution. Luckily, both enjoyed a similar and aligned interest. They did not have oodles of money; they were struggling in a sense. Whatever they saved came after they had spent some money on these kids. Nihal expanded some more: 'We used to have parties for the kids from the orphanages, bring them home for cakes and balloons. Those were the days when you had these little projectors for presentations at the office. I used to take the projector home (with permission) and show the kids films and cartoons at home.'

Happy and conscious choices

From what Nihal said to me, it appeared that taking care of street kids was a sort of ingrained habit from childhood for him and Shyama, like they were taught to brush their teeth, to look clean and to pray.

'We used to go looking for kids on the street during difficult periods, like in winter. In those days Bombay had cold winters, with the temperature frequently dipping to 10 degrees. We used to fill our Fiat car with blankets from Crawford Market and go out looking for kids on the pavement and give them those. We also used to get food packets and distribute them.

'Shyama and I were not exactly well-off at the time. But we decided that, while we would not live our lives in misery, we would choose the things we would spend on and would go big on those. The first thing we had to do was save a little bit. The second was to set aside something for people who were weaker than us. Thereafter, we would focus the balance on something we valued. Neither of us had any interest in clothes and accessories, so we would buy the cheapest, and that's how it remains to this day. The shirt I'm wearing now—and I wear only white shirts—costs just £5 in London, whereas my son-in-law wears £40 shirts. Till recently I used to wear a very functional Titan watch; now I have a Timex that costs all of £18. My shoes are always inexpensive and I have never had a suit stitched; they were always off the rack. And Shyama is the same.

'But holidays were important for us. Entertaining, food and wine, those were things we would spend on. It was a kind of focused indulgence. The quality of our home was also important for us, so we would really spend on that. In the early days it was difficult. For instance, in our very first home, in Chennai, I remember we had no money for even a coffee table. So we unscrewed the doors from the built-in cupboards, covered them in cloth and mounted them on bricks. People thought our coffee table was artistic and started to copy what we were doing.

'Entertainment and travel were the things we spent money on. We didn't spend money on watches, jewellery, shirts, saris and the like. Neither of us inherited anything from our families. Many years later, Shyama got a flat from her mother, but other than that we never received from our families.'

I asked Nihal whether he and Shyama actually sat down to discuss these aspects, or whether the dots got connected by some intuitive process.

NK: No we didn't talk about it at all. In fact, I often wonder how much of my life was accident, how much of it was intuition and how much of it was planned. I am inclined to conclude that very little of it was planned. A lot of it came out of intuition, out of accident. Now I can see some threads here which I didn't see before: for example, this habit of choosing one difficult question in an exam paper to answer thoroughly, choosing travel, home and entertainment and eschewing everything else. When we went for something, it was always a 110 per cent effort, while ignoring the rest because the rest did not matter.'

I found this pattern repeated in Nihal's personal choices, home choices and family choices. What about the professional?

NK: There too, absolutely. When I was successful in Indonesia as chairman, as you can imagine, and especially with the good network and relationships at the top, there were any number of offers to do other things. I said, 'No, I am doing my thing here. So I am going to stay with this because I am not interested in any of other roles in Unilever. Let me do this thing which I am enjoying, which I want to do.' That is what took me to St Jude.

The glimmer of an energising purpose

When we got back to India, we wanted to do something with this abiding interest in children. We used to send money to needy children from our overseas postings, but now that we were back we wanted to not duplicate something which someone else was doing. How did we come to the idea of St Jude?

We used to see advertisements in the newspapers. For example, the son of a farmer from somewhere would die of cancer because he and his family did not have the money for treatment, so I used to write small cheques and contribute. One day I went to the office of one of these charities. I asked them for their donor list and they gave me four telephone directories full of people giving Rs 100 a month. I asked what was missing. They said a safe and loving place to stay. They said that holistic care was missing. These kids come with their parents from Bihar, Orissa, Uttar Pradesh, Madhya Pradesh and elsewhere. About 70 per cent don't even find the doctors willing to treat them because they are beyond the treatment stage. They are sent into palliative care, which is the management of pain, till they die.

RG: *What took you there in the first place? Was it again the accident of donations?*

NK: That's right.

RG: *I thought the fact that your maternal grandmother died of cancer may have taken you there. But, from what you say, it was not cancer that drew you in.*

NK: No, no, not at all. It was to chase down this origin of doing good stuff and it happened to be cancer. And I was very impressed that there were not just a few big names and big sums, but everyone donating little bits. I thought about what was missing and they told me this: the families lie on the pavement outside and pick up all kinds of infectious diseases.

I went to see some of the so-called *dharamshalas*. Most of them had been built for 120 people but accommodated 650. These people were crowded in the filthiest of circumstances; it was worse than living on the pavement. They would surely die from tuberculosis or pneumonia or bronchitis or some infectious diseases that they would pick up.

RG: *So St Jude was not a pre-mediated mission that brought you back? You came back and St Jude happened?*

NK: Absolutely. I learnt about their abandonment of treatment, because these people would get fed up and go back. There are only a few months left for the child and, so, let the child die in the village. I talked to the doctors and they said the same thing about what was missing. And then on one paediatric cancer day, I went to the Tata Memorial Centre when all these kids were there; all bald, all wearing masks, and I was sitting there in the audience at the hospital. They invited me to the stage.

On that stage—I don't know; there must have been a hand

above me at that moment—I made a commitment. When I was asked to speak, I said I was going to work to see that no poor child from a village or small town, coming into a big city like Mumbai looking for treatment, will go without a clean, safe and caring place to stay. I made that commitment.

RG: *And you did not have a clue?*

NK: How to do it? Not a clue! Everyone told me I was completely mad—and I had said free of cost. How could I do this in a place like Mumbai?

RG: *It was purely impulsive?*

NK: Accidental, intuitive, impulsive, whatever you call it. And so the hand above sent me to see Julio Ribeiro [the former police commissioner of Bombay]. His daughter, Anna, an interior decorator, was the person who did up our flat in Mumbai while we were abroad. She said: 'Go talk to my dad.' Her dad, Julio, said, 'Nihal, I am the chairman of the Bombay Mothers & Children Welfare Society and we run hospitals and crèches for the needy. Will you come on the board? I said, 'Yes, it links very much with what I want to do?' He said they had this dilapidated place in the BDD *chawls*. 'You go and see it and if you can use it, then we'll give it to you.'

I went and saw it and my heart sank. It was in bad condition but the other members of the team we had put together asked me not to worry, saying that they would get it done up. This was in December 2005-January 2006; by the end of March we had our first centre. At that stage I had decided that everything that I had learnt during my forty years at Unilever, I was going to invest in this thing. There were three things I was going to invest in after retirement. First, I was not going to undertake professional consultancy but I would do non-executive directorships. Second, I was going to take everything I had learnt into my non-executive roles. Third and last, I was going to take all that I had learnt also into building an organisation called St Jude, which would have the same cutting-edge quality that I had been taught. I put all I knew into St Jude, whether it was designing standard operating procedures, attention to quality or safety management. Every single thing that I learnt I put there, which is why it runs like clockwork even when I am not there.

The recipe that I formulated at Unilever Indonesia was, incidentally, used by an author friend as a title for his book, *Think Big, Start Small, Move Fast*. I put that into St Jude as well. We thought big, we planned to start with eight family unit centres, and we are not going to move to the second centre until we got the model right. For the prototype centre I said I don't want any funding, because the salary from my last year at Unilever was put entirely into that. That's how we funded it and it took twenty months to get that model right.

RG: *What did you have to do to make the place right?*

NK: Julio gave possession to me immediately, but it had to be renovated. We put a team together for that. I had heard Tim Smit when he came as a guest speaker to Unilever. Smit was famous for a project in Eden in the United Kingdom, where he took an old mining site in Cornwall and made it into the largest tourist attraction in the country. He had some unique 'key performance indicators' for his team: they had to wish each other 'good morning' every day, they had to learn to do the samba, they had to find out what a fellow colleague wanted but couldn't get—what his dream was—and quietly make sure that that dream came true.

In forming the St Jude team, too, we had different key performance indicators. We said they all had to be third-generation friends, their grandparents had to be friends, their parents had to be friends and they had to be friends. Then we said that apart from

Shyama and me, who were geriatrics, the others must be under fifty. Then they all had to have non-transferable jobs and they had to be professionals: lawyers, doctors, accountants, etc. It was a small team and we identified them through word of mouth. Those who were third generation had only a few degrees of separation, so it all came together. If you take the lawyer on the team, for example, the senior Diwanji was Shyama's father's parents' lawyer. Shishir Diwanji was looking after matters pertaining to Shyama and me, and now Jai Diwanji and his brother, Apoorva, are Mallika's friends. The starting team had nine members.

I said to the team, 'Look, before I tell you what I want from you, let me tell you what I do not want from you. I want to tell you that I don't want any money from any of you. Money is in the bank. I don't want to go and ask anyone for money because there are enough people asking.' Our model was going to be 'show and don't ask'. Let the potential donor ask, 'What can I do?' Then you can tell them but don't ask anyone for any money. Show them the brochures or, preferably, show them the centres. Don't ask anyone for any money. 'It will come,' I told the team, 'just trust me, it will come.' And, sure enough, it has come. Of course, once it comes you follow up and remind people and all of that, but in the beginning we never asked.

RG: *How did you develop skills to convert the BDD chawls into suitable premises?*

NK: A lot of it came from people not just giving money but their skills and their time. There were a lot of professionals in the team and the team began to grow. There were architects, contractors and all such professionals who came in. There was a bonding and an alignment of people; the rest of it fell into place, especially the money part.

Was it an intuitive thing or was it a deliberate, planned thing? It was intuitively the right thing to do. It came out of seeing other people doing the wrong thing, as well. I had seen a number of charities that would approach me, take the money and disappear; and I would never hear from them again. I was sure we were not going to be like that.

Humanity is a universal religion

I was also inspired by Mother Teresa, who never asked anyone for any money. Money came because of the work she was doing. Well, let the work speak for itself. Do something which is so outstanding that the money will come. That, honestly speaking, is how it has been going. Even now, in our dealings with the Tata Medical Centre, it's all about what they see. We show them the model and it is a good model.

Mother Teresa had another influence on me: her secular nature. When Albania reopened its first mosque after years of Communist rule, they invited Mother Teresa to open that mosque. The Catholic Church was up in arms and the Vatican tried to stop it. Mother Theresa wrote to the Pope and said, 'I am going to do this and the reason I am doing this, your Holiness, is because I want these people to come back to God first. We'll then tell them about Christ, but let them first come back to God.'

That ecumenical nature of things was again an inspiration for me and St Jude. The way I saw it, these people come from an atmosphere of inequality in their villages: there are Brahmins, there are Harijans and there are Muslims. They won't walk on the same side of the street, but we are going to teach them equality. We are going to build on the fact that their pain can unite them. We are going to teach them equality that they can then take back in caring for others. That is one of the huge things that has come out from St Jude, and I got that from Mother Teresa.

RG: *St Jude is indifferent to caste and religion?*

NK: Totally and honestly. Many of these people you see in the family rooms, on their shelf is an altar and there will be a small picture of St Jude there next to their Hindu god. They have come to believe that this is a divinity that helps those in desperate need of help. There is no specificity about religion and that was the influence of Mother Teresa. She was a devout Catholic. She was a nun. She had absolutely no proselytising zeal to turn everyone into a Catholic.

Enjoying work and family

RG: *You don't seem to view any conflict between work and family. The inability to balance and make choices destroys marriages, people relationships and careers in ways all of us can see.*

NK: In the initial stages, I thought I was going to face a struggle. But that struggle never came, and that too at any cost. I am a great believer in what you said. I am a great believer in and-also rather than either-or. I discovered quite early on that this work and life balance is a gimbal-mounted thing; it's not a seesaw of work and family. There is a third dimension to it which leads to this gimbal mounting, and that is the person—ME. So it is work, family and me; it is about striking a balance with these three. I sacrificed a lot of 'me' in this process.

As a result, I guess I am not going to live long as I could have. I have certainly had to put up with a whole lot of maladies and not am the healthiest person you know. I have given up exercise, sleep, any number of healthy ways. I certainly had to give up a lot of 'me' time. People consider me to be foolish to, at this stage of my life, devote the amount of time I do to St Jude, to the amount of time I spend in my non-executive directorships, on travel and work.

I have always tried to spend quality time with Mallika. You may not know about these holidays I have been taking with Mallika since she was six-seven years old; only father and daughter and it continues to this day. Earlier on it was once every five years, then we made it every three years, now it is almost once every two years as the tape runs out for me. We go off together for anything between five and eight days to a strange place. We have been to Iceland, we've been to Turkey, to Cyprus, we've been to Jordan, we've been to Jaipur and we've been to Jerusalem. We share the same room, we spend time together 24x7. Earlier it was without her mother, now it is without her husband and kids.

I do it because—I'm going back to when she was six—I used to spend so much time on my work that I did not have enough quantity time with her. The way I chose to balance that was to make up for it in quality. It is during these days that we talk freely with each other. There is nothing else during these days except her for me and me for her.

RG: *So you crafted uniquely distinctive solutions that suited you and your family. And you're not prescriptive—and, luckily for you, it worked.*

NK: I was always looking for those things. I'll give you another example. I want my grandchildren to remember me in some way. Now, you can do that in many ways. The way I have chosen to do it is to build for them a wine cellar, with about 30-40 cases. The first case of this wine will be ready for drinking when they were eighteen years old and the last case will be ready when they reach sixty. In between there are seven-eight cases for all the milestones in their lives. They will be there and I will be no longer around; and they will know that this has come from their Papi. It is my way of giving them a lasting memory of me.

Importance of longstanding relationships

RG: *Are you a longstanding-relationships type of person? What influences that?*

NK: You know, my sister was not in any way influenced by my parents' divorce. I was hugely affected. She was two years younger than me and she took to my stepfather. She was not in any way fazed by that divorce, but I went through hell. If I were to choose one of the five worst periods of my life, one was when my mother died (which I have still not got over) and another was when my parents split up. I never wanted that to happen.

I never wanted the severing up of joyful relationships in any sphere of my life, whether it was at work or in marriage or in friendships, never. That mind-set had a deep influence on me. This is my 70th year and as a gift my former chairman at Unilever had a mass for me at Westminster Cathedral. The whole Cathedral was closed, they had a small mass in the crypt, then a private tour of the Cathedral and then dinner. Paul Polman and his wife were there, so were Niall and Ingrid, and among the people who attended was John Downham, whom you will recall I met from my market research days. I meet him at least once a year or once in two years (he is ninety-one years old now). He has had both his hips replaced, he has had three cancer operations. He came to my retirement party and, a decade later, to my 70th birthday function.

There are friends from my work life and from my student life. This year I'll be hosting a dinner for my school class of 1959, where various friends will attend. Some of my friends from then are no more but those that remain will gather at my home.

My friendship with Rajesh Bahadur has also lasted. Rajesh was my first boss and he remained my boss throughout my life. No matter who else I worked for, I was always working for Rajesh. He taught me how to write and it was hard, you know. He would make me hone and sharpen every sentence. He would send back the draft ten times and make me rewrite it. He taught me how to write. He taught me how to present. He taught me never to say what was on the slide because people could read that. He taught me how to play bridge, he taught me how to make wine, and he taught me about integrity in business and about ethics in business. He taught me how to look at the human side of a situation and not be a harsh judge, looking at it only through the prism or lens of biases and prejudice. I was in the United Kingdom when my mother died and he did everything for my mother's funeral. In fact, when I came back, he handed over to me the keys of the coffin in which she was buried. One of the greatest things I owe you is the fact that—when I was not here when Rajesh died—you made the speech and I was deeply concerned as to who was going to do that.

RG: *You exude a sense of having had a complete life in which you made your own choices and are able to live happily with those choices. What would you say to people? How do you achieve completeness?*

NK: There are different levels. I have not thought about it but, while you were speaking, I was thinking. I think there is very much the analogy of the Maslow hierarchy. I feel fulfilled that I planned my finances well, so that my wife, daughter and Smita will never want for anything. That's a huge fulfilment for me. And I can tell you that that was not the case with the previous generation.

One level up, I think I find great fulfilment in seeing the values that Mallika has. And these are not sort of physical; it is not about having money in the bank but a set of values. For this I am grateful, and even more so because she does not have some of the faults that I have and which I have struggled to suppress. That for me is a huge completeness.

I also find, at yet another level, a great fulfilment in the lives of the people whom I feel that I have touched, particularly so since I have been privileged to touch the lives of a large number of people. They keep in touch with me like I keep in touch with you, Gopal. Quite often when they have a question and they come to me for an answer—that for me is fulfilment. Finally, a couple of things that I built have lasted: Unilever Indonesia is one and St Jude is another.

Hard work, luck and the hand of God

On the 75th anniversary of Unilever, in 2005, Nihal was invited to give a speech to the assembled leaders of Unilever. He opened his speech by saying he felt a bit like Chauncey Gardiner. 'Chauncey was a gardener, played by Peter Sellers in the 1979 movie *Being There*. Chauncey spent his whole life tending his master's garden, until he got injured in an accident that brought him into the home of a Wall Street tycoon. There he met the beleaguered President of the USA. Mistaking Chauncey for one of the host's powerful financial colleagues, the President asks desperately for Chauncey's advice on what to say the next day about the country's stagnant economy. Caught in the headlights of the President's reference to the 'bad season on Wall Street' Chauncey states calmly, 'In a garden, growth has its season. There are spring and summer, but there are also fall and winter. And then spring and summer again. As long as the roots are not severed, all is well and all will be well.' Amazed by the profound simplicity of the statement, the President uses the idea in his speech with great success.'

RG: *Can you say something about the Nihal that went to Indonesia on the second occasion around year 2000? That Nihal was very different from the Nihal who went in 1984 for his first stint in that country.*

NK: You are absolutely right, Gopal. Without any question and, in a sense, I think if you use the gardening analogy somehow, the things I seemed to do there seemed to bear fruit much more than anything that I would have got had I gone gardening elsewhere. I cannot tell you why that is so. I cannot tell you that it is for this reason or that; it just happened. I think that it has as much to do with them as with me.

In the 1980s I was your predecessor as general manager (exports). I remember my exports stint as being all about me. After my first six months in Indonesia on the first stint, a chap called Asikin Suryadharna sat me down and said, 'Nihal, you know I watched you in the first three-six months. The way you were going about it, I bet you wish you had six of your crack troopers from India here with you to do this job.' I said, 'Yes, how did you guess?' He said, 'Wrong, what you want to do is up to you but if you don't do it within the mores of Indonesia, it's not going to last; it's going to fail.' I then found that somehow people there were responding to me, and in a way that made me change hugely.

I left India in 1984 a hugely individualist person. I left Indonesia in 2005 for the second time a team player with some 'Jim Collins level 5'. I left with very much more; I learnt those level 5 things during that Indonesia experience.

Nihal feels that there were many aspects of his second stint in Indonesia that helped transform him as a person. One worth mentioning is the setting up, during his tenure at Unilever Indonesia, of the Peduli Foundation (ULPF), which means Unilever Indonesia Cares. ULPF was the corporate conduit to execute four legs of corporate relations: sustainable clean rivers, sustainable small and medium enterprises, sustainable fisheries, and sustainable public health. This strategic move concentrated and replaced the large number of ad hoc charity programs of the company.

RG: *Although your career lasted 40 years, the real flowering of a purpose happened during those six years in Indonesia. About 15 per cent of your professional time accounted for 90 per cent of your emotional flowering, and you had not planned it. So, when you think back, your life is a series of dots; you're not sure who connected what and when. The dots got connected in a manner that makes you a complete human being. There seems to be lots of people involved in there.*

NK: And that continues. There are influences but there is no need for you to connect the dots; the connections somehow grow.

RG: *And yet more people, including you and me, early in our career have been psyched into learning or thinking, or have been told explicitly to design and plan what you want to be. Why does it take to reach age sixty or so to realise that?*

NK: There is only one thing that I did plan and I planned very intentionally and that was the fadeout from Unilever. I knew that I was never going to be able to transition successfully from being the chairman of Unilever Indonesia into the next stage of my retirement, as understood normally. I knew that I needed a fadeout and so I negotiated this period to allow me the fadeout and the parallel tracking into the next stage. I would never have been able to move directly from the last day of office as chairman of Unilever Indonesia into the next stage of my life. I am glad I did that, very glad.

RG: *Wonderful, Nihal, you have a book in you and I don't know why you are not doing it.*

NK: Not that I haven't thought about writing a book but, honestly Gopal, it's not my thing. Book-writing is your thing; my thing is St Jude. I was there day before yesterday, spending hours with kids and the new managers from Jaipur, Hyderabad and other centres. They are here for induction training and I was at the Willingdon Club, sitting on the lawn, chatting with them, telling them about other centre managers, telling them about myself, what to look for and what to expect, chatting with them because they are the future. That's my thing.

RG: *I reckon, at the end of the day, each person has to do what drives him or her.*

5

A Theory of Career and Life

'The little emotions are the great captains of our lives and we obey them without realising it.'

—Vincent van Gogh

In the first two chapters, I narrated why I wrote this book and what it is about. In the third and fourth chapters, I recounted the story of a PLU (person like us) called Nihal Kaviratne. His narrative demonstrated how commonplace and small-looking episodes shaped him and his life-views; how his mind-set and character evolved; how he became extra-sensitive to suffering; how he grew up as neutral to religion but got committed to humanity as a virtue.

Episodes that appear minor at the time of occurrence chisel away at an individual's mental make-up, quietly and constantly. They shape the individual to whom the episode has happened. The effect of such chiselling is the update of the person's 'theory of life.'

A theory of life

Professor Clayton Christensen of Harvard Business School

argues that you are constantly trying to develop a theory, which really means to establish a cause and effect. You know that your brain processes what you see and sense. Your brain leads you to formulate a theory which tries to connect a cause and an effect. Then you formulate a theory, which you test through subsequent experiences.

For example, I have often been asked by students from less-known colleges about how they can overcome the disadvantage of not being from an IIT or IIM. The question arose in their mind because of the common perception that if someone graduated from an IIT, that person is likely to be better than an engineer from a lesser institution. Such a perception in the interviewer's mind creates a positive bias for a candidate from a premier institution appears alongside a candidate from a lesser institution.

In science, an example of a theory is that no matter how many times you drop a ball, it will fall—theory of gravity.

When I meet young managers on the subject of professionalism, they observe that businessmen who earn wealth quickly have the practice of cosying up to politicians. If their competitor grows faster than them through certain practices, the young professionals assume that being close to politicians is essential for success. As they gain further experiences, they test the learnings against their theory that political proximity is essential for business success. If the hypothesis or theory seems to hold, then it influences their future actions as well as interactions with the world. As they grow, they might gradually become aggressive with political networking and corrupt practices in their quest for success: all this because they have developed a theory for business success.

To elucidate his idea about theory of something, Clayton Christensen (*How Will You Measure Your Life,* New York, 2012) cites the example of flying. Early researchers thought that feathers and wings were essential to fly. So they spent a lot of time designing and trying different feathers and wings—to no great avail. Feathers and wings had a high correlation to flying, but did not provide the basis for a theory.

In 1899, Wilbur Wright assembled all the useful works on aviation from the Smithsonian. After consulting hundreds of weather reports from the American Meteorological Bureau, Wilbur and his brother, Frank, selected Kitty Hawk, North Carolina as the experimental field. The brothers spent three years experimenting with rudders and controls before they put an engine on a plane. Finally, after postulating and modifying their theory of flying over and over again, at 10.35 am on 17 December 1903, the world's first ever powered flight occurred for all of twelve seconds. This is the power of theory!

Whatever learnings you may have in life, for sure, one learning is likely to be the identical among all people—that no two people perceive life, its incidents, experiences and people, in the same way. There are infinite vignettes about success, career and relationships.

During my professional career of forty-eight years, I have worked with several bosses, colleagues and subordinates, many of whom I can recall distinctly. However, my memories of the association with them do not precisely match their memories of our association. I learnt this when I recounted certain incidents and episodes involving them while writing my earlier books. In some cases they recalled the details differently. In some others they could not recall the episode at all.

Likewise with the siblings I grew up with. Although we were all born to the same parents and we grew up in the same house during approximately the same period, and although we are able to recall common occurrences, our memory of the episodes vary considerably. My younger brother recalls my petulant fights with him as vividly as I recall my elder brother bullying me, but in both cases our memories are different.

If there is a reality to an episode, then it is intriguing that there are so many varying memories of the episode. And it is these memories that shape our assumptions about life; emotions become markers in our personality, for example, a happy versus sad childhood, or easy success versus struggling for success.

'Inside Out' film—emotions organise our life

Our educational and social upbringing instil into us the virtues of rationality. Rightly so. However as the Vincent van Gogh quotation at the beginning of this chapter states, it is the little emotions of our life that become the captains of our lives and we listen to our emotions instinctively. Psychologists who have researched this subject feel that emotions actually organise and guide our lives. Emotions are not the disrupters that they are assumed to be.

Dacher Keltner is professor of psychology at University of California and Paul Ekman is professor emeritus of psychology at the same university. Their research suggest that six emotions guide our lives—Joy, Anger, Disgust, Sadness, Fear and Surprise. In their article ('The Science of "Inside Out",' *International New York Times,* July 3, 2015), they describe how 'emotions organize—rather than disrupt—rational thinking…the prevailing view in western thought has been that emotions are enemies of rationality… emotions guide our perceptions of the world, our memories of the past and even our moral judgments of right and wrong.' The two professors in fact advised writer and film director, Pete Docter, when he embarked on his new Pixar film titled 'Inside Out.'

Six lenses

We judge events and people all the time, even though we may not be conscious about it. But what influences our judgment? In reality what we observe is reconstructed by our brain through the chisel of our own experiences. That is how we make judgments.

To get a layman's sense of how people actually do this, I adopted a heuristic process and talked to many people.

I asked the question: 'What words come to your mind when you judge what a successful and fulfilling life is?'

The responses had to be one or two words only, not long sentences. I got a huge number of words and expressions in response. I wrote down the adjectives and nouns used by individuals to represent their concept of success and fulfilment in life. I then categorised them into single words which I, as a person, could make sense of. That is how I conceived of the model of six lenses.

One thing is common among all of us: everybody seeks success and fulfilment. It does not matter that there is no universal or even personal definition of what constitutes success and fulfilment. The quest for success is a key lens that influences our 'view of life' on the spectacle frame.

The narrative about Nihal Kaviratne provided examples of how one person sought success and fulfilment in his life. Nihal and Shyama adopted their distinctive ways by reflecting on events and people; by validating what was important to them; by updating their hypotheses or mind-sets about a fulfilling life with new insights. In this way they could align their future actions with their mind-sets as altered by the view through their lenses.

Nihal waited for many years to find a calling in life, a true purpose. He let the purpose evolve rather than get restless through an artificial or forced search. In terms of managing a tight income-expenditure balance in the early years, rather than seek quick-fix methods or let ambition go wild, Nihal and his wife, Shyama, made choices on what they would spend on and what expenditures did not matter to them.

Their family backgrounds made two things important for them: first, their mutual relationship, which they assiduously nurtured, as also the relationship with their daughter; second, a constant engagement with care and charity. They both decided, as it were, that they needed to be authentic to themselves, and that they would do what it took to be so. They valued the lucky breaks they got and cherished these with the logic that they were from the 'Hand' above.

Nihal faced up to the need to make choices, for example, by giving up a Harvard educational opportunity to get married, by not seeking fresh postings after his second Indonesia stint, and never to dwell on the past or whether he did the right or the wrong thing.

Reading well-written accounts of others' careers and life stories offers inspiration to an individual with regard to the dilemmas that inevitably arise throughout one's life.

Assumptions and mind-sets

Leadership dilemmas and related events during our life pose multiple questions. For example, if I work in a company, are my ideals and goals aligned to those of my company? Does my company live up to the professed ideals of its leaders? Does my boss come through as truly transparent with people? Does my organisation take what I think to be rational decisions? What is a purposeful life for me? What is courage? How does one get fulfilment in life? What is ethical behaviour?

If you had to seek comprehensive answers to each and every such question, you cannot lead a sane life. You may do with shallow and practical answers to most questions, but will seek deep answers to a few questions. That is why you need a mental model to simplify life. You have built a mental archetypes of good behaviour, a sort of personal standard of conduct. Against this personal standard, you observe and judge events and people. Your observation and judgment influence your standard and your actions, and also vice versa.

To develop a practical model, something that would help me think through the dilemmas of work and life, I conceived of the model of six lenses.

Purpose is your mind-set or belief about your life's aim. It is a long-term goal, which, if pursued, could give the ultimate happiness. It does not mean that the person has found the goal easily or has nurtured the goal for a long time.

Authenticity is the mind-set or belief about who you are at the core. Around that belief, you build ideas about truthfulness, frankness, speaking your mind, and self-confidence.

Courage is a mind-set about things you admire, such as ambition, boldness, resisting unfair power, taking risks, and facing up to your vulnerabilities.

Trust encompasses virtues such as reliability, never letting anyone down, keeping secrets, loyalty and faith.

Luck is also a mind-set or belief. You may believe in luck in some form or the other. You may pretend you don't believe in luck, except when it suits you. It includes words such as fate, unexpected fortune, providence, unearned luck and fluke.

Success and fulfilment is the belief about what gives satisfaction and contentedness. It is about being happy, radiating positive energy and enjoying what there is rather than cribbing about what there isn't.

The view through each lens has meaning and relevance for every one of us. They appear to be independent but they are connected, a bit like the parts of our human body.

Few of us are exposed to philosophical thinking and reading. Therefore our knowledge of philosophy is fairly limited. There is pragmatism in our daily living; it is not consciously based on any lofty platform of philosophy or elevated thinking. We inherently accept that virtue and happiness are two sides of the same coin. We also accept that talking about a positive life and actually living a positive life are quite separate things.

Leading a positive life

So what is this positive life on which we build our happiness? There is a 1980s HBS case study entitled *The Parable of the Sadhu*. It concerns the dilemma of a New York merchant banker, who was nominated to an outbound leadership event. Part of this program was a group-climb in the Himalayas. On a cold morning, as the team set out for what looked like a strenuous and final assault, the protagonist was shocked to hear a groan from the ice. Upon looking closely he found an emaciated and groaning sadhu lying on the path. The protagonist was assailed with doubt—what should he do? Should he save the human life and, in the process, abandon the adventure, or carry on with the hope that someone else would save the sadhu?

The Harvard class participants, who were dominantly American and European, felt that it would be right to abandon the climb and save the sadhu. One Indian participant seemed to agree, but only 'in principle.' She pensively wondered about the reality of life, whereby she, or her countrymen, did not do so every morning as they left their houses in Mumbai or Delhi. There are too many similar situations which Indian city residents encounter on a daily basis! She reflected on the reality that her response in Boston was different from her actions in her real life.

The message is that context matters. Relativities do matter—in this instance, and in most instances.

Consider an example relating to ethics: to speed up clearances, your employer may consider it as unacceptable to bribe a public-service official on behalf of the company. However, in your personal context, if you are buying some land or a flat, you may, even if with some discomfort, agree that some 'speed money' be paid and recovered through your lawyer's or contractor's bill. These are contradictory and confusing behaviours that we try desperately to reconcile.

Consider another example relating to hiring: you have found an excellent marketing chief after a long search. Everything looks right about his competence and his intellect. On his personal side, you note that he has separated from his wife. His personal life may not be orderly, by your standards. Do you follow your logic or your intuition? You then realise that you can use logic as far as the 'logic road' takes you, but the final decision has to be taken intuitively.

How much reconciliation of confusing images we need to make is exemplified by the dilemmas evident all around us.

I exemplify the six lenses through the illustrative dilemmas suggested by their narration. These are drawn from history, mythology and management.

The paradox of purpose

In an increasingly competitive world, we are constantly told that people with a clear purpose succeed. Successful people, we are further told, are so focused that they seem to have no option but to succeed. People with a purpose get focused very early in their lives. Many experience an 'aha' moment in their life that turns out to be transformational.

But the vast majority of humanity spends an entire lifetime seeking a purpose. Many die without knowing what their purpose was in life. Or so it appears to an observer.

Roger Federer started playing tennis at the age of three, when he was gifted a racket. He is supposed to have instantly felt that this would be the passion of his life. Federer's sense of purpose and focus enabled his success. True or false? It is the truth, but not the whole truth. Because it does not tell the story of many more three-year-olds (like me!) who did not make it to the tennis hall of fame and whose tennis life stories have not been written.

In the 1890s in South Africa, Mohandas Karamchand Gandhi

held a first class train ticket from Durban to Pietermaritzburg. He was on a lawyer's mission for his client, Dada Abdullah. He was thrown out of the train by an apartheid-influenced railway inspector. Gandhi found his life's purpose in that moment. He became determined to fight discrimination and injustice. That journey led him on to win independence for India. True or false? It is the truth, but not the whole truth. Surely there were many other influences on Gandhi subsequently. What about many other travellers who were discriminated against? Their stories have not been written.

In the late 1800s, John Watson, a resident of Castle Carrock in North England, set up Watson Hotel at Bombay. The hotel boasted India's first steam-powered elevator, 120 rooms with fitted baths and a ventilation system of *punkawallahs*. It was meant for exclusive use by Europeans. The Indian industrialist Jamsetji Tata and his European friend were denied entry into the Watson Hotel, Bombay. Jamsetji vowed to set up a rival, world class hotel which would allow Indians to enter and use its premises without prejudice or discrimination. He did do so and he set up the Taj Mahal Hotel. Through that incident, Jamsetji found his purpose in life. True or false? It is possibly true, but certainly not the whole truth.

Your life purpose is your unique identity. One person's purpose cannot be compared to another's. To each person, his or her purpose is the basic and purposeful reason to live.

Until the age of forty, Muhammad was deeply engaged in the caravan trade in and around Mecca. He was successful and was distinctive for his smart commercial ways. Influenced by the *hanifs* (monks) who lived around Mecca, he sometimes undertook *tahannut* (an ascetic meditation) in solitary vigil in the mountains around Mecca. During the month of *Ramadan* in the year 610, Muhammad went to Mount Hira and something special happened to him. He achieved an altered state of consciousness when he received a message. He felt a sense of terror and awe as he received the message. His purpose in life was thus established.

The first person of Indian origin to be canonised by the Pope was Gonsalo Garcia. He was the son of a Portuguese man and an Indian mother, born in 1557 in Vasai (also known as Bassein) near Bombay. Gonsalo's life's purpose and accomplishments were distinctly his. He became a Jesuit. At the age of fifteen, in 1572, he persuaded his mentor to let him go to Japan as a missionary. Gonsalo later joined the Franciscan order. In 1596, the Japanese shogun ordered Gonsalo and two other missionaries to be executed. On February 4, 1597, at 10 am in Nagasaki, Gonsalo was held up on a cross and executed by spearing. He was first venerated and later canonised by the Church. His memory is kept alive through a college in Vasai that is named after him.

Is purpose important for an individual? What exactly is its role? How do you know when you have got a purpose?

The ambiguity about authenticity

Sri Rama was, of course, the model human being. He was the epitome of perfection, virtue and authenticity. If Sri Rama's actions were to be viewed through the lens of authenticity, then his supreme virtue becomes evident. Did he not accept fourteen years of banishment to the forests of Dandakaranya instantaneously? Did he not do so in a trice, at the very moment that his father asked him to do so? Did he not do so cheerfully, never once showing anger or disappointment that his father had got conned into implementing a boon given in a totally different context? Sri Rama was, and continues to be, the epitome of authenticity.

Yet, after the Lanka War and the rescue of Sita, a strange episode occurred. When his followers questioned his wife, Sita's, virtue, Sri Rama agreed to put her through the test of fire to establish the truth. When Sita emerged successfully from the test of fire, a washer man continued to express scepticism. Based on this scepticism, Sri Rama banished Sita to the forest.

How could an 'authentic' person do these kind of things? What is authenticity?

The charisma of courage

In the Mahabharata, Bhishma was the epitome of virtue of all kinds and of the highest variety. His courage and his commitment to his word were legendary. He promised his father that he would never marry, stake a claim to the throne, or produce an heir who might do so. He stayed true to that promise through his virtuous life. He had vowed that he would never kill a woman. On the battlefield, the only way by which Arjuna could overcome Bhishma was to accept Lord Krishna's advice: to allow Shikhandi to appear before Bhishma in the battle as a woman. As expected, Bhishma laid down his arms and allowed himself to be killed by Arjuna's arrows. Of such nobility and courage was Bhishma made. Intriguingly, the courageous Bhishma was present in the Kaurava court when the Pandava princess, Draupadi, was insulted, molested and disrobed. One word, just one word of disapproval from the patriarch could have brought the vulgar situation under control. What did Bhishma do?

First he commented on the piteous plea of Draupadi, who was being scorned and molested in open court. She asked Bhishma, 'How could Yudhishtira gamble on me? Did he lose his mind before he lost me?' It was an important question, because if Yudhishtira was not of firm mind at the time he made his wager, his bet on Draupadi could be questioned. Viewed in that way, Bhishma conceded in the court that Yudhishtira may not have been of firm mind. But he went on to state that the wife was the inalienable property of the husband (valid in those days, certainly abhorrent today). Hence Yudhishtira had the right to wager Draupadi in the game. As a result of this obtuse logic, the molestation continued—and Bhishma kept quiet. Draupadi's torment was eased only when she called out to her Lord Krishna for help. Lord Krishna solved the problem by making an unending cloth get draped around Draupadi, who could not hence be disrobed.

Why was the ever-so-courageous Bhishma quiet? What is courage?

The twist with trust

In the Mahabharata, Karna is in many ways an admirable character. He was the illegitimate son of Kunti, who subsequently gave birth to the five Pandava brothers. Neither Karna nor the Pandavas knew of their relationship, which Kunti had kept secret for long. Like the infant Moses was left in a wicker basket, the unwanted baby Karna too was left in a wicker basket by Kunti. The baby was found by a charioteer (of a lower caste) who raised the child with love. Karna came to be known as a Sutaputra, a charioteer's son.

As he grew up Karna sequentially gained the attention, admiration and trust of the Kauravas. He became an exalted and trusted person in their court. Later in the epic, the Kauravas are arraigned against the Pandavas in battle, and so, unknowingly, Karna is pitted against his own half-brothers.

At a certain time in the denouement of the story, Karna learns from Kunti that she is his real mother and that the Pandavas are his half-brothers. That made the Mahabharata war a sort of fratricide. Karna is shocked by this revelation. Kunti hoped that Karna would leave the 'enemy camp' of the Kauravas. Karna declined to do so, reasoning that the Kauravas had trusted him for long. He could not let them down. Of such strong character was Karna made. But Karna also had his prejudices.

Through his growing-up years, Karna had acquired strong negative feelings about Arjuna, the middle brother among the Pandavas. Arjuna was reckoned to be a superior archer, as evidenced by his winning various archery contests. Arjuna had stood out during the *swayamvar* to win Draupadi's hand. It was an event Karna wished to compete in, but could not due to his low caste. Due to his deep jealousy of Arjuna, Karna had vowed that one day he would kill Arjuna.

Long before such a day came, Karna had the opportunity to show his hugely negative and prejudiced feelings in the Kaurava court when Draupadi was being disrobed by the Kauravas.

Karna, the epitome of trust, heckled Draupadi. Referring to her as the wife of many men, he suggested that she was effectively a person of low virtue. He quoted an ancient rule, 'A woman with more than four husbands is nothing but a public woman, a whore.' Disrobing such a person was not wrong. Saying so, he encouraged the courtiers to continue with their dishonourable act.

How can one reconcile Karna's undoubted virtue and trustworthiness with his seemingly cavalier attitude and behaviour in the Kaurava court? If the trustworthy Karna acted with Draupadi in the manner that he did, then what is trust?

The lure of luck

It would appear that there is no concept of luck among the world's major religions or philosophies.

In Islam a person who has faith is strong. He has a courage that can challenge the whole universe. 'A person whose senses of reliance on Allah, and whose consenting to whatever comes from Him are weak, relies on inessential, pointless and vain things such as luck, stars and horoscopes,' one scholar has stated.

In Christianity, too, there is no acceptance of luck per se; rather, good occurrences are manifestations of God's Hand. In the Book of Ruth, a widow named Ruth cares for her widowed mother-in-law, Naomi. On one occasion, Ruth goes to earn grain by working in someone's field. Ruth earns a lot of grain that day, much to the surprise and happiness of the mother-in-law. The field belonged to a tribe called Elimelech, to which Ruth's father-in-law had belonged. The mother-in-law, Naomi, did not regard this event as a chance. Naomi says, 'The Lord bless him, He has not stopped showing His kindness to the living and to the dead. That man is our close relative; he is one of our kinsmen.'

Lord Buddha believed in individual responsibility, rational thought and social obligations rather than fears and irrational superstitions. He did not believe in luck, fate or chance. He taught that whatever happens does so due to causes. There is the story of a high caste man who discards his expensive cloth in a local cemetery because it has a rat bite, believed to be a harbinger of bad luck. Later, he hears that the Buddha has picked up the cloth and is using it. He runs after the Buddha to warn him to discard the cloth. The Buddha tells him that he alone can bring upon himself good or bad circumstances. So the Buddha keeps the expensive cloth.

In the Bhagavad Gita, Lord Krishna enunciates the doctrine of karma. He says, 'Regardless of consequences and without worrying about success or failure, you must do your duty at all times.' The law of karma also states that there is a connection between every cause and effect, even if we do not understand the connection. The carrying forward of your account book of good and bad deeds into the next birth, and the important role of rebirth are essential parts of the Hindu psyche.

Saint Ramanuja expresses the philosophy of surrender (*saranagati* or *prapatti*), through which the devotee surrenders all of his or her actions to God and performs his or her duty with zeal and faith in God.

If every religion expresses the same view, and we know that

religion does shape our beliefs and behaviour, how did the concept of luck or fortune come to dominate our thinking? Humans have invented the term in order to enable themselves to understand the dichotomies they encounter in their everyday lives. It is a persuasive explanation for phenomena they cannot comprehend.

How come one person gets a disproportionate raise in salary, an out-of-turn promotion or hits the jackpot for wealth? Luck (maybe good or bad) offers an explanation that reduces our bewilderment. The concept of luck and fate, consequently, simplifies the search for a comforting answer to complicated questions.

The secret of success

Every life must be driven by ambition. Yet everybody must also lead a whole life in perfect contentment. There is a natural tension between ambition and contentment. Sometimes the balance tips towards ambition, especially when one is younger. At other times, especially when one is older, the balance tips towards contentment. At the end of any life, the cup of accomplishment and contentment are both half full. The epitaphs and eulogies thereafter are based on the half-full cups of what has been accomplished. The empty half cups of non-accomplishment are interred with the person's ashes.

It is every ageing person's deep desire to die peacefully, having lived a life of fulfilment and contentment. But to judge whether the life has been fulfilling creates its own dilemmas of judgment. Do you need to be well-known, even famous? Can an 'ordinary person' live as fulfilled a life as a 'famous person'?

When I read about the Mahatma Gandhi's life, I am unable to resolve the question of whether he led a fulfilled life. He changed the trajectory of life for more than half a billion of the subcontinent's people through his struggles and personal sacrifices. He died surely knowing that he made a huge difference to the existence of so many people, all within his short lifespan.

Yet, in terms of his family life, the Mahatma could not have had a feeling of happiness and fulfilment. There were many moments and incidents of great distress to him as a father. Was he an adjusting husband who discharged his Vedic vow of 'treating his bride as an equal partner and like a queen in his house?' (Incidentally, many people do not realise that that is the precise vow every Hindu takes during a Vedic wedding ceremony.)

How can we think about fulfilment in life as a balance between work and family?

The story of Bhishma is one of the most celebrated in Indian mythology. During the battle of Kurukshetra, Bhishma is struck down by the arrows of Arjuna, his grandnephew. The arrows pierce his body and when Bhishma falls down from his chariot, the arrows form a bed so that Bhishma's body does not lie on Mother Earth. He dies on that bed of arrows, but only after some deep philosophical conversations and after reciting his views on life. The spiritual *Vishnu Saharanaam* is recited by Bhishma while lying on his bed of arrows.

With his body resting on the bed of arrows, Bhishma's head hangs loose with no support. Bhishma asks Arjuna to provide some support. Arjuna does so by piercing three arrows in the ground in so a manner that Bhishma's head can rest on those arrows. A satisfied Bhishma says, 'What a fitting pillow for a warrior like me—a pillow to match the bed.' He then asks for water. Arjuna again pierces his arrows into the earth and cool water springs out of the hole and goes directly into Bhishma's mouth. Bhishma is satiated.

Thanks to a karmic boon, Bhishma is aware of all of his earlier births. He feels he had committed no sin through all the many rebirths he has had. He asks Lord Krishna why he is dying with such suffering in spite of his track record of good karmas. Lord Krishna reminds him that in one birth he had sinned by inflicting pain on insects when he stuck needles and thorns into their bodies. This sin, coupled with his unjust support of the Kauravas, caused him that painful death.

It is a great gain to feel fulfilled with life. This means one must be thankful for all the good things that happened, must not be regretful and must be forgetful of the bad things that happened. There should never be remorse about the positive things that could, or should, have happened. This can cause only bitterness. Bitterness and fulfilment do not go hand in hand. If Bhishma had a fulfilled life, what can we learn about 'fulfilment' in life?

Human quality

In this book I lay a lot of emphasis on the human quality, the effect of learning from experiences. Human quality, embodying the lessons of life, are so well-known for so long that zillions of books and articles have been written about them. They are all available freely in the 'Human Knowledge Bank'.

Yet each person has to learn life lessons for himself or herself as he or she goes through a personal odyssey of discovery about work, life, friendship and relationships. Although the Human Knowledge Bank is accessible to all, everyone does not seem to bank on or with it.

Furthermore, the availability of such knowledge is not of any great value as compared with learning that knowledge by oneself! The lessons of experience in life and in management work in the same way. You know the lessons but are unable to always practise them.

Every person's personality has two elements, a base and an overlay. Together they constitute the complete personality of the individual. The base is about temperament, which is more or less fixed by a person's genes and circumstances of birth. The overlay is the human quality, which is shaped by the person's life experiences.

Temperament plus human quality equals the personality. What follows are five examples about human quality.

Acting under the pressure

There is an award-winning 2014 Swedish movie entitled *Force Majeure*. The film presents a week in the life of a holidaying Swedish family in the French Alps. The family comprises Tomas, his wife, Ebba and their two kids. On the second day of the holiday, as the family lunches on the outdoor deck, a controlled and planned avalanche seems to go awry. The avalanche starts to look real. The lunch parties fled the deck, and so did Tomas. Luckily there was no disaster, but Ebba feels that Tomas ran away to save himself instead of thinking about his family. The whole movie is about Ebba's feeling of being let down and Tomas's defence of his actions. Commenting on the film in *The Guardian*, Julian Baggini invokes Aristotle's wisdom, 'To become good, you have to practise being good by cultivating the habits of goodness. Only then will you find yourself doing the right things automatically.'

Gathering and scattering

The second human quality I consider is that, approximately, the earlier part of career and family seems to be characterised by 'gathering', while the later part is about 'scattering'. Gathering refers to acquisition or accumulation of all sorts of things: money, assets, influence, power, status and creature comforts. Scattering refers to the progressive deployment of the gathered stuff: settling children, assisting family and friends, sharing, even if selectively, the fruits of acquired things like influence and power. Everyone's life, or almost everyone's, has a gathering phase followed by a scattering phase. Phases of these kinds have been eulogised and described by philosophers for centuries, as, for example, the four *ashrams* of life according to Indian tradition and the eight stages of life according to psychologist Erik Erikson.

The narrative about Nihal Kaviratne epitomises this human quality.

Work and relationships

The third pattern is that the tension between work and influence, on the one hand, and family and enjoyment, on the other, settle into a sort of equilibrium that is uniquely suited to the concerned individual. It is almost that a realisation dawns that you cannot have it all, whether you are a man or a woman. You learn to balance the demands of career and family, based on questions like who you are, what your purpose in life is, and what brings you happiness. You are sure that you have got it all wrong initially. Even if you are not so sure, your wife and kids will remind you that you should have given them more time in the early years. When you think you have achieved a better balance, the family's needs have changed!

Circles of interest

The fourth pattern concerns the concentricity of our life circles of interest with others' life circles of interest. Romance and marriage books push us to believe that ideal partners have common interests. Early on in any marriage, the impracticality of such a thesis is made apparent. So a pattern of targeted concentricity starts to develop. As the family becomes bigger, more circles come into play through additional members and interests. When the couple becomes empty nesters, the circles can be quite different and distinct, almost in preparation for the inevitable, when each circle will submerge into the infinite in its own way, and singly so, as it came initially.

The certainty of uncertainty

The fifth and last pattern I will refer to is the relevance of Werner Heisenberg's uncertainty principle to work, influence, family and enjoyment. Heisenberg's principle states that you can never determine the exact position and speed of an atomic particle, hence some degree of uncertainty in the relative position of atomic particles is inevitable. This is because in order to detect the particle you have to shoot another atomic particle at it, a bit like sending a red billiards ball to find the blue one on the table. The mere act of the particles colliding has the effect of changing the speed and position of the target particle before the collision. The same happens with life. We chase, say, wealth throughout our life. But as soon as we have acquired it we have to think about what to do with it. As one of India's richest men once told me, 'Gopal, it is a curse to have too little wealth, but it is also a curse to have too much.' Likewise, the acquisition of power leads us to the question of what exactly to do with that power.

That explains the old Shakespearean adage: 'Uneasy lies the head that wears the crown.'

The journey of career and life has some purpose. It is to be happy: to give all one has, to take all one can, and to keep both in balance. When we refer to happiness what we really mean is a complex phenomenon called emotional well-being. To be happy is to possess a favourable emotional state. It is not about money, influence and possessions.

It is this path to happiness that motivates human beings to seek a life of virtue.

Seeking fulfillment

Life's biggest lessons are learnt from the tiniest of creatures.

One Sunday morning, a contented man sat in his balcony.

A little ant caught his eye; it was travelling from one end of the balcony to the other, carrying a leaf several times bigger than itself. He saw that the ant, when faced with impediments during its journey, paused, took a diversion and then continued towards its destination. At one point the tiny creature comes across a crack in the floor. It stops for a while and then lays the huge leaf over the crack, walks over the leaf and picks it up on the other side. The man watches this for about an hour, until the creature has reached its destination—a tiny hole in the floor. Now how could the ant carry into the tiny hole its large leaf? It simply couldn't!

So the minuscule thing —after all the painstaking work and the exercising of wonderful skill, after overcoming all the difficulties along the way—leaves behind the large leaf and goes home empty-handed. It is a day on which the ant learns a great lesson. Isn't that the truth about our lives as well?

We don't quite realise in our life's journey that these are just burdens that we are carrying with utmost care while being fearful of losing them, only to find that at the end they are useless and we can't take them with us.

For most people a good life is one that leads to a circle of virtue. Aristotle had posited that virtue and human happiness are synonymous. He had argued that we all try to develop inner strength and virtues. Without those strengths and virtues we cannot be human.

For sure most of us wish to lead a good life. But what is the good life?

Quest for happiness

Happiness is the new buzz subject. Men are no happier than women and people in sunny places are no happier than those in chilly places. Beautiful people are no happier than ugly people and hugely successful people are no happier than less successful people. Happiness books and happiness seminars are among the fastest-growing businesses. But it all comes back to sound common sense. Happiness is tied to giving rather than taking, to volunteering and to donating, to having a happy marriage and to being connected with siblings and people.

It is apt to recall Vincent van Gogh's letter to his brother in July 1880:

> 'One cannot always tell what it is that keeps us shut in, confines us, seems to bury us, but still one feels certain barriers, certain gates, certain walls. Is all this imagination, fantasy? I do not think so. And then one asks: Is it for long, is it forever, and is it for eternity? Do you know what frees one from this captivity? It is very deep, serious affection. Being friends, being brothers, love that is what opens the prison by supreme power, by some magic force.'

As van Gogh implies, we are prisoners of our own unhappiness and we can set ourselves free of our confines through deep, serious affection. Life often seems to bestow its bounties at the wrong time on the wrong people. Banks lend to those who are creditworthy, which means that they have quite a lot of money to repay. Good and rich food is easily accessible to well-fed folk, who use gymnasiums and weight-loss plans regularly. When one is of the age and has the inclination to go on a honeymoon, one is most likely strapped for cash. And when one has the cash one may not be in the age bracket for a honeymoon.

My grown-up children have a naughty laugh when my wife and I traipse off to New Zealand or on an Arctic cruise.

6

Purpose: The First Lens

'Man has a great need to know whether it is worthwhile to be born, to live, to struggle, to suffer and to die...and whether it is worthwhile to commit oneself to some ideal which is superior to material and contingent interests...whether there is a why that justifies his earthly existence...giving a meaning to his life and to his journey.'

Pope John Paul II, 1979

In the previous chapter, the idea of lenses through which we view people and episodes was elaborated. All human beings seek success and fulfilment, even though each person might describe differently what these words mean to him or her. In seeking success and fulfilment, the basic human need to know what the purpose of life is provides the first lens. It is a critical view.

Purpose in life and career is a significant force. It represents the driving vigour in the individual. It provides life-giving power to each individual, just like the engine of an automobile gives power to the wheels through the gear box and other parts of the car.

Do I want to be a rich industrialist or a great philanthropic for whom wealth and industry are a means to an end? Think of

John D. Rockefeller, the founder of the Rockefeller Foundation; William Hesketh Lever, the founder of Unilever; or Jamsetji Tata, the founder of Tata.

Do I want to be a fabulously successful surgeon or do I want to spread succour to those whom my surgery might help? Think of Dr S. Badrinath, the founder of Shankar Netralaya.

Through my participation in industry, do I want India to be economically advanced or do I want Indians to be happy people? JRD Tata said he would rather see 'a happy India' after he was invested with the Bharat Ratna.

My colleague the late Russi Lala used to say, 'If your search for a purpose is with yourself in the centre, you may run around in circles for a long time, but if it is focused on other people or a cause beneficial to your fellowmen, you may find your destiny sooner...you will never find a higher purpose until you look beyond yourself to the needs of others.'

Thanks to my close association with two wonderful companies, Unilever and Tata, over the decades, I developed a deep interest in the subject of corporate purpose. Why does the corporation exist? What is its purpose? Where lies the balance between the focus on owner enrichment versus societal good? How can an organisation be run so that it is long-lived?

One book, titled *Purpose* and authored by Nikos Mourkiaginnis, a senior partner in an elite consulting firm called Panthea, delivered to me significant insights. The author's focus is on corporate purpose and it relies on a heady mixture of philosophy, corporate stories and leadership lessons. I was much influenced by this book and wish to state this influence at the beginning of this chapter, in which I explore the personal purpose of individuals in relation to their existence.

Allocating your time, talent and energy

When you view events, options and people through the lens of your purpose in life, your brain processes the theory of your life, what you really want to do. You then allocate the only three resources you have to fulfil that purpose—your time, your talent and your energy. In short, every person has enough time, talent and energy to do what he or she *really* wants to do in life. This is the manner in which you create a strategy for your life.

The truth is that almost everybody is potentially a greatly accomplished person. In the course of accomplishing the chosen purpose, that person may end up as a happy person or a troubled soul. The examples below suggest how two very accomplished people who may have become very troubled souls. Their purpose in life and their quest for success was thwarted by the actions that they took.

Vincent van Gogh

Vincent van Gogh was a creative genius, a post-impressionist painter whose work was notable for its beauty, emotion and colour. During the second half of the nineteenth century, van Gogh made an enormous impact on the world of art through his paintings. He had no formal training in painting. His younger brother, who had a business as an art dealer, supported him financially. Van Gogh took lessons on his own and studied books.

Van Gogh's personal life appears to have been far from wonderful. During his growing-up years his family struggled to earn enough money, and young Vincent had to start working at the age of fifteen at his uncle's art gallery. When he grew up, he had a catastrophic love life, being constantly attracted to women in trouble, first a widowed cousin who felt repulsed by him and, later, an alcoholic prostitute who became his mistress. It was his art that helped van Gogh stay emotionally balanced.

If you view van Gogh's life story through the eye of his works and his accomplishments, he led a glorious life of great influence. If you view it with the eye of his relationships and his enjoyment of life, you may form a different opinion. It is not necessary for us to pass judgement on van Gogh's life, but we do so with regard to the people we encounter in our daily lives. That judgement may or may not be fair, but it is what influences your perception of that person.

Kawas Nanavati

The second example is from a story that captured the hearts and minds of Indians during my schooldays. It pertains to a dashing and handsome naval officer called Commander Kawas Manekshaw Nanavati. Born in 1925, Kawas joined the Indian Navy and worked as defence attaché to the Indian High Commissioner in London, V.K. Krishna Menon. As a result he came into some acquaintance with the Nehru-Gandhi family. Kawas had married an English lady by the name Sylvia. They had two sons and a daughter. The good-looking couple and their family had settled in Mumbai in a building opposite to where my parents lived.

Kawas had to travel frequently for his work, leaving Sylvia and the children at home. In April 1959, upon return from one of his assignments, he found Sylvia aloof and distant. Sylvia confessed to an affair with a friend of fifteen years, Prem Ahuja. On that same evening, Nanavati dropped his family at the Metro cinema for a movie, then excused himself to confront Ahuja. He went to the naval base and collected his pistol and found Ahuja in his flat. When Kawas asked him whether he intended to marry Sylvia, Ahuja apparently responded, 'Do you think I will marry every woman I sleep with?' This presumably infuriated Kawas, who used his pistol to settle the issue. Whatever the details may be, Ahuja died in the encounter. The murder trial aroused great public interest and emotion. It also raised many complex questions concerning the law and ethics. Kawas served a sentence but was released after three years. The Nanavati family went away to Canada, where Kawas died in 2003. What appeared from the outside like a dream family in the mid-1950s had a very difficult time for the rest of their lives.

It is quite stimulating to think that there is not just one fact for each event. Yet we lead our lives as though that is so. For example, if a person has been convicted of murder, we are accustomed to think that he must pay for it. We feel that way because he is seen to have exercised free choice in performing the act of murder. But was his really a free choice or were there other contextual influences which restricted that choice. The Nanavati case threw up such questions.

Individual purpose is a blend of five aspects

The important feature of individual purpose is that it is designed by that individual from conscious choices that he or she exercises. Purpose is not something that just happens to a person; it is what the individual designs (albeit unconsciously) to represent who he or she is, and what that person wants to achieve in life. It can be to change the world with intellectual contributions. It can be to influence the world through humanities and art. It can be to create wealth. It may be to uplift society. It can be to achieve harmony within the self.

It is helpful to think of individual purpose as being a self-designed blend of five things:

> *Humanistic*: I want to influence for the good the affairs of people and society. It may be through music, art, entertainment, social service or even spirituality. I stand for certain principles in the way I live and those are important to me.

- *Honorific*: I want to earn respect by pushing the intellectual frontiers of human consciousness. It may be by creating new knowledge and insights. It may be through science, technology or new inventions.
- *Historic*: I must leave an impact on the times I live in. It may be by doing things that will be remembered in the future. It may be by winning sports records, by ruling long, by being seen as bold. It matters a lot to me how others think of me.
- *Hedonistic*: I want to create a great life for myself and those whom I care for. It can be through acquiring wealth, power, influence and a pleasurable life. It involves a hint of being focused on self.
- *Holistic*: I am not trying to change the whole world. I want to be a great human being, a good citizen and try to do the right things all through my life. I must be a balanced and responsible member of my society and community.

If you can think of these five aspects as a sort of pentagon, then each of them is represented by one of the points. An individual is represented by his or her own diagram—very individual and distinctive. And it is that person who has, consciously or unconsciously, designed the spider diagram.

It is important to appreciate the subtleties around purpose by considering a few examples of PLUs with out-of-the-ordinary purposes and actions as they pursued their purpose.

Father Victor Courtois—uniting Muslims and Christians

This is an example of a person who scored high on 'humanistic' on the five pentagon points.

From my days at St Xavier's School, Calcutta, I vaguely remember a Jesuit called Fr Victor Courtois. He was in the school for a short time, but his was a striking figure: short, chubby and with a deep red beard. Strangely, he spoke Urdu. He died in 1960 and his body was kept in the school chapel for some time. I recall him as a jovial Catholic who loved Islam and Muslims for reasons I could not appreciate. Many years later, I found a reference to his life story in a publication by the Goethals Indian Library, Kolkata.

Fr Courtois was born in Louvain in Belgium in 1907 and he joined the Jesuits when he was nineteen. He was assigned to work in India in 1931. To prepare for his sojourn, he studied books, among them some on Mughal rule in India. This chance acquaintance aroused in him a lifelong purpose: to bridge the gap between Muslims and Christians.

He went to Beirut, Damascus, Cairo and other Arab cities to learn classical Arabic and to prepare himself for full-time work in Muslim-Christian relations. He wrote scholarly papers, researched and established an institute in Calcutta to advance knowledge on the subject. He devoted his life to helping indigent Muslims and to furthering Christian-Muslim relations. He wrote, 'The study of Islam should lead to greater love and better appreciation of Muslims... We should understand not what separates them but what can bring Muslims and Christians together... We study them not as enemies, but as brothers and sisters.'

From all accounts, it would appear that Fr Courtois died young (at fifty-three), but with a sense of humanistic accomplishment, a serenity of having done what he loved to do, and feeling fulfilled with a holistic life that he designed for himself by exercising choices at different points of time.

William Shockley—brilliant but impossible

Here is an example of pursuit of an 'honorific;' purpose.

I first read about William Shockley when I was an undergraduate engineering student. Along with two other scientists, he had won the Nobel Prize for his work on transistors just a few years before I was making my choice of studies. Of course, I knew nothing about Shockley as a person, but his accomplishments as a scientist were certainly inspiring to me and were an influence in the choice of electronics as my main subject. I learnt more about Shockley later in my life, particularly reignited through Michael Malone's book, *The Intel Trinity*. I was fascinated to read that Shockley, a brilliant scientist, worked at Bell Labs. Along with John Bardeen and Walter Brattain, he worked on doping non-electrical conducting material with germanium and silicon to establish that it could be a conductor. This laid the basis for the transistor revolution and the chip revolution. Shockley went on to establish his own company in 1953 so as to gain commercial benefits from his invention.

Shockley was as brilliant a scientist as he was a poor manager. He arrived in the Bay Area with every chance of high success. He, first, rigorously interviewed and assembled eight fine and upcoming scientists. Among them were Robert Noyce, Gordon Moore and Andy Grove, who felt greatly honoured to be recruited by a famous scientist into his company, Shockley Transistor Laboratories, to develop transistor technologies. Shockley turned out to be paranoid, contemptuous of subordinates and hugely arrogant. He was a tyrannical boss, and such a poor leader that all the eight people working there walked out of the company. They set up Fairchild Semiconductors and, subsequently, Intel Corporation.

Shockley was pig-headed in many matters and he treated his bright, young people with scant regard. He behaved as though the eight were trying to undermine him. When, in frustration, all eight walked out, he called them 'the traitorous eight'. When he was ousted from his own company, Shockley joined the Stanford faculty. He became interested in distracting race matters and dubbed blacks as less intelligent than whites. He was called a

'Hitlerite' by a reporter and that remark caused him to get into a libel suit. Shockley won one dollar as damages, but his reputation was in the mud by the end of the suit.

Shockley died of prostate cancer in 1989, almost completely estranged from all his relatives and friends. His children were reported to have learnt of his death through the newspapers.

My student-day hero's spider diagram may perhaps show a score high on 'honorific' and 'historic', medium on 'hedonistic', and quite low on 'humanistic' and 'holistic'.

So why did Shockley botch up what seemed a great purpose?

Bob Kearns—self-destructing or single-minded

Here is an example of a person who pursued a 'historic' purpose.

Early in his life, Robert (Bob) Kearns had been a high school cross-country athlete, an outstanding violinist and a teenage intelligence officer in World War II. Kearns had a doctorate in engineering and had taught the subject for eleven years at Wayne State University in Detroit. He grew up near the giant Ford plant in River Rouge, Michigan, and always thought of the auto company as a place that welcomed someone with ingenuity.

But from 1976, his sole focus in life was to battle the auto giants and reclaim his invention. 'I need the money, but that's not what this is about,' he told *Regardie* magazine in 1990. 'I've spent a lifetime on this. This case isn't just a trial. It's about the meaning of Bob Kearns's life.'

Kearns got his idea on his wedding night in 1953, when a champagne cork struck him in the left eye, which eventually went blind. The blinking of his eye led him to wonder if he could make windshield wipers that would move at intervals instead of in a constant back-and-forth motion. After years of experiments at home and on his cars, Kearns believed his invention was ready. He applied for patents, mounted his wipers on the 1962 Ford

Galaxy and drove to Ford's headquarters to demonstrate his novel product. Later in 1967, he received the first of more than thirty patents for his wipers

Ford's engineers had been experimenting with vacuum-operated wipers, but Kearns was the first to invent an intermittent wiper with an electric motor. Ford engineers swarmed over his car, at one point sending him out of the workroom, convinced he was activating the wipers with a button in his pocket. At the end of the meeting, Ford told Kearns that they would revert to him. However, Ford did not do so and, in fact, stopped answering his calls. Kearns was left on his own.

In 1969, Ford came out with the first intermittent wiper system in the United States, followed within a few years by other automotive manufacturers. In 1976, Kearns's son bought an electric circuit for a Mercedes-Benz intermittent wiper which Kearns took apart, only to discover it was almost identical to what he'd invented. He had a nervous breakdown soon after. Police picked him up in Tennessee and his family checked him into the psychiatric ward at Montgomery General Hospital. When he came out after a few weeks, his red hair had turned white.

All he wanted, he often said, was the chance to run a factory with his six children and build his wiper motors, along with a later invention for a windshield wiper that was activated automatically by rainfall. In the end, his courtroom battles cost him his job, his marriage and, at times, his mental health.

Kearns filed suit against Ford for patent infringement in 1978, seeking $141 million in damages (a figure eventually raised to $325 million). In all, he filed lawsuits against twenty-six car manufacturers and other companies. Kearns supported himself with disability pay after his breakdown and by trading in foreign currencies.

By the early 1980s, his wife had had enough. 'It had become an obsession,' recalled Hall, who lives in Arizona. 'I told him, "I can't stand this life." He said, "This *is* my life."' When their divorce was granted in 1989, Kearns was in the midst of his court case against Ford.

After twelve years of litigation, Ford finally offered to pay Kearns millions of dollars to settle the case. His attorney at the time, William Durkee of Houston, estimated Kearns could have received at least $50 million from Ford and comparable amounts from other carmakers. Kearns refused the offer.

'He wanted to be a manufacturer and supply that system to the automotive industry,' said Richard L. Aitken, a Washington patent lawyer who had worked with Kearns since the 1960s. 'That was the most important thing to him.'

In July 1990, a federal jury ruled that Ford had unintentionally infringed on Kearns's patent and awarded him $10.2 million. After the Ford settlement, Kearns turned his sights on Chrysler. In December 1991, a federal jury ruled that Chrysler had infringed unfairly on his patent. Firing his law firm a week before the damage phase of the trial, Kearns argued his case and was awarded more than $20 million. Chrysler appealed to the Supreme Court, which ruled that Kearns was entitled to the money but rejected his argument that Chrysler should be prohibited from using his design.

Having gone through five law firms, an exhausted Kearns was unable to manage his multiple lawsuits on his own. When he missed deadlines for filing papers in his cases against General Motors and German and Japanese auto companies, US District Judge Avern Cohn, who presided over all of Kearns's trials in Detroit, dismissed the remaining cases.

By then, Kearns's patents had expired, having passed the seventeen-year window of ownership then in effect. He bought a house on the Wye River, near Queenstown on the Eastern Shore, and entered an uneasy retirement. From time to time, he would call his children and his attorney and talk about reclaiming his patents.

When Bob Kearns died of cancer at the age of seventy-seven in February 2005, the *Washington Post* described him as an accomplished but frustrated inventor. 'Robert Kearns's battles with the world's automotive giants have come to an end. Kearns devoted decades of his life to fighting Ford Motor Co, Chrysler Corp and other carmakers in court, trying to gain the credit he thought he deserved as the inventor of the intermittent windshield wiper,' the *Post* reported. Kearns carried his lonely fight all the way to the Supreme Court, one man against the might of the industrial world and a patent system he believed had let him down.

When he died at seventy-seven, of brain cancer complicated by Alzheimer's disease, Kearns had gained some vindication in the form of $30 million in settlements from Ford and Chrysler, but he never got what he had always sought.

Sarah Marquis—testing her limits

Here is a final example of a person who pursued an 'honorific' purpose.

The New York Times reported the story of Sarah Marquis (September 25, 2014) and her case illustrates her choice of purpose as gleaned through the story. Sarah grew up in a village of 500, Montsevelier, in the Jura Mountains in Switzerland. She had lots of cousins through her parents' seventeen siblings. The family was obviously a big, screaming one, but for her it was a nightmare. She grew to enjoy some solitude and wanderlust. At the age of eight she ran away into the woods with her dog and spent a night alone in a cave. Later, as she grew up and began work in a travel company, she felt challenged by the thought of whether she could survive by herself in nature.

Sarah decided to ride a horse across Turkey, where she ate apricots off trees and slept with the saddle as a pillow. She undertook a trip to New Zealand's Kahurangi National Park without food to see if she could survive thirty days in the wilderness. 'That was the first time I got in touch with the wild,' she would recall. She canoed through Canada's Algonquin Park without learning the techniques of canoeing. She went alone to Patagonia and was attacked by beavers. She walked 8,700 miles around Australia. On her 38th birthday in 2010, she set out to walk through Asia from Siberia and all the way to Australia.

The news report about Sarah lists many challenges which she undertook, describes the unbelievable hardships she overcame and how she set up tougher and newer challenges for herself. In her trip photos, she appears filthy, her hair like a dirty nest and her eyes beseeching and introspective. In real life, it is reported that she is beautiful and charming, always sporting a generous smile.

The territory that Sarah explores is internal, as one can gather: the nature of fear, the limits of stamina and self-reliance. She feels that the experience of extreme travel is fantastic, provided you don't die. 'My happiness increases tenfold,' she wrote.

A reader might rate Sarah's purpose as very high on honorific and historic, medium on humanistic and low on hedonistic and holistic. That could just be her spider diagram. It has been designed by her and there is nothing great or poor about it.

Feeling rewarded through hardship

I was amazed to read about a German, Wilfred Thesiger, who undertook a number of gut-wrenching, life-threatening expeditions across the *Rub-al-Khali*, the empty quarter of Arabia. Thesiger's team suffered freezing night temperatures, intense and searing day temperatures and chases by bandits. Yet Thesiger reported that he found the whole experience 'very satisfying'.

In their book (*Extreme: Why Some People Thrive at the Limit*, New York, 2014), Emma Barret and Paul Martin draw from psychological studies as well as the first-person accounts of extreme adventurers. British mountaineer Joe Simpson fell into a crevasse in the Andean mountains and spent three agonising days crawling to safety with a broken leg. John Hanning Speke explored the African bush in the 1850s, searching for the origin of the Nile. When a beetle crawled into his ear, he stuck a penknife into that ear. He badly damaged his eardrum and his face got all swollen. Geologist Natalie Cabrol explored a volcanic lake in South America at an elevation of 20,000 feet above sea level. She endured extreme cold and hypoxia but claimed that 'this was the most rewarding experience of my life.'

No single explanation brings out the motivation of such people. Some want to make history, others to contribute to knowledge, some others crave status and yet some others want to escape boredom and drudgery. Thrill seekers are buzzed on a complex personal cocktail of traits. According to research, there is a part of the brain which gets activated by anticipation of pleasurable experiences such as sex, drugs and entertainment. It is precisely this part that gets activated for people with risk-taking behaviour—as happens with a corporate chief executive on a trail of hubris or other such adventurers.

Purpose is a personal odyssey

For the large part of humanity, the search for purpose is incessant. The search must be within oneself. However, Like the Himalayan deer seeking from outside the source of its musk odour, people too often seek purpose from the external.

Russi Lala had told me and the Nihal Kaviratne story illustrates that when you search inside and see how you can help others, you start to see the light. It can be said that the sense of personal purpose has certain common characteristics:

> It is fugitive. You are not sure you have a purpose and, if so, what it is.

- It seems to change over the cycle of life. It is influenced by events and people during your life.
- Even if articulated, it seems to be ordinary and unworthy of being written about.
- It seems unworthy compared with the dramatic purpose espoused by the likes of Mahatma Gandhi and Nelson Mandela.

Yet it is the most important source of energy that drives your life. The conclusion has to be that for your purpose to be important only you need to know it. Only you need to grapple with the dilemmas and design your own purpose, little or great. In fact, it may be said that ordinary people with no illusions of fame and grandeur follow their own purpose; it is just that some become famous and well-known. But the less known need not be perceived to have no purpose, or an uninstructive purpose.

7

Authenticity: The Second Lens

'But yield who will to their separation, my object in living is to unite
My avocation and my vocation as my two eyes make one in sight.'

—Robert Frost, 'Two Tramps in Mud Time'

INSEAD Professor Herminia Ibarra opened her *Harvard Business Review* article (Jan-Feb 2015) with the words, 'Authenticity has become the gold standard for leadership. But a simplistic understanding of what it means can hinder your growth and limit your impact.'

Astonishing? Bewildering? Maybe, but absolutely spot on, and true.

For many people, considerable mental turmoil in relationships arises from their perception of the authenticity of the folks who feature in their lives. The way you perceive others' authenticity is the basis of giving or receiving trust in human relations. A boss or colleague who acts true sometimes and is shifty and unreliable at others is a source of confusion and personal anguish. A work colleague or neighbour whose true goodwill for you is unclear or variable causes tension and grief; in extreme cases, such a feeling leads to insecurity, temper outbursts and even suicide.

Amazingly, the same person and the same episode are viewed

vastly differently by different people, because they use different lenses to make their judgements. A relevant example is political leadership in any country. The president or prime minister of almost every country is viewed as being pretty much authentic by some people and vilified as being the opposite by others. Think of George Bush II, Tony Blair or even Narendra Modi.

That this situation occurs with 'famous and great people' is chastening to the plain and simple folks whom I address through this book. It even happened with Mahatma Gandhi.

Alternate view of a great person

In his scintillating book (*Nehru and Bose: Parallel Lives,* Gurgaon, 2014) historian Rudrangshu Mukherjee traces the parallels between Jawaharlal Nehru and Subhas Chandra Bose through the years of the freedom struggle. They are traditionally depicted as opposites or foes, but the author demonstrates the many similarities in their opinions, but with different action outcomes. Gandhi naturally emerges as a central figure to both.

Nehru and Bose, individually and collectively, did not agree with Gandhi on quite a few occasions and matters. But their ways of reconciling the facts and responding to the situation were quite different. Bose and Nehru viewed the Mahatma differently on the same events and also made different judgements about the authenticity of the Mahatma.

In March 1931, when the civil disobedience movement had already been launched by the Congress, Gandhi was a party to the Gandhi-Irwin pact. The Mahatma directed the Congress to end the civil disobedience agitation. Nehru was in Delhi and watched the developments from close quarters. He was crestfallen. In his autobiography, Nehru wrote with great frankness, 'The thing had been done, our leader had committed himself; and even if we disagreed with him, what could we do? Throw him over? Break from him?'

With regard to Bose, it is first worth recalling the conversation between Viceroy Irwin and Mahatma Gandhi about the man. According to Irwin's records, Gandhi had included Bose's name among the Congressmen who would accompany him for the talks. However, according to Gandhi's account of the same meeting, Bose's name 'came up'. Gandhi had said, 'He is my opponent and will denounce me; still, if he wants to attend, we must let give him a chance to do so.' As it happened, Bose was in prison when he learnt about the pact. He was deeply disturbed and in complete disagreement. But considering Gandhi's overpowering popularity, Bose let the matter pass at that time.

Bose went to Vienna soon thereafter for medical treatment. By mid-1933, he heard about new developments, including the cessation of the civil disobedience movement. He issued a statement from Vienna which stated, '...as a political leader Mahatma Gandhi has failed. The time has come for a radical reorganisation of the Congress on a new principle and with a new method.' Bose became despondent about the developments in India and wrote to Kshitij Prasad Chattopadhyaya, a dear friend from his Cambridge college days, '...The path is long and dreary... It is not the bright future alone which calls but the gloomy uncertainty as well... There is pleasure in travelling—in groping—also in falling.'

In his book, *The Indian Struggle 1920–1942* (Bombay, 1964), Bose unambiguously stated his view about Gandhi's leadership, 'Gandhi has rendered and will continue to render phenomenal services to his country... India's salvation will not be achieved under his leadership...he is fundamentally a reformist, not a revolutionary.' From Austria in 1937, Bose wrote his autobiography, covering the period from his childhood up until then, under the title *An Indian Pilgrim: An Unfinished Autobiography and Collected Letters, 1897–1921* (New York, 1965). In this book Bose wrote about his belief in his spirit (which to him meant working with conscious purpose through time and space) in the following terms: 'It is a pragmatic necessity. My nature demands it...I have an increasing purpose...I am not a mere conglomeration of atoms.'

An event then occurred which shook Bose's confidence in the Mahatma. In 1938, the Bengal Congress, after the elections, sat in the opposition to a coalition ministry of Fazlul Huq. The coalition was not quite working and Bose had mooted an alternative alliance for the opposition Congress. Bose had had several conversations within the party; he knew that the Congress, including Gandhi personally, supported his idea. Bose was, in the circumstances, shocked to receive a letter dated December 18, 1938 from Gandhi opposing the Congress coalition idea. It was not clear to Bose why Gandhi had changed his position, but most likely it must have been the influence of some inner coterie advisors. Bose made it clear to Gandhi that 'if you do not reverse your views, I would have to carefully consider my position.' In the twilight of his political career, Bose made it clear that he could not be pushed beyond a point, Gandhi or no Gandhi. By that time a pattern had emerged that on such points: Nehru would yield to Gandhi but Bose would not.

Soon after, in January 1939, Bose contested for the presidency of Congress against the choice of the high command, Pattabhi Sitaramayya. Bose won the election. Gandhi reacted in a manner that was considered to be devoid of grace: he issued a public statement that the defeat of his candidate, Sitaramayya, was tantamount to a personal defeat for him. This act of taking a fair election personally upset Bose greatly. Author Rudrangshu Mukherjee has commented, 'Gandhi emerged from this episode at his worst: petty and given to machinations, the archetypal Tammany hall politician, his moral posturing notwithstanding.'

What further proof is needed to confirm that the perception of authenticity depends on the lens through which you view the episode and the person?

Authenticity is doing what you have to

I found the story of Captain Carlsen very relevant. What he regarded as his plain and simple duty was viewed by others as an act of great heroism. Which was the authentic Captain Carlsen?

Just after Christmas in 1951, the thirty-seven-year-old Captain Carlsen's ship, *Flying Enterprise*, was caught in the worst Atlantic storm in fifty years just off the coast of England. For two weeks the world awakened each morning to hear on the radio what happened to the ship. The captain had ordered his entire crew of forty and the ten passengers on board to abandon the ship.

As the main man on the ship, Captain Carlsen felt that he had to remain on board as long as she remained afloat. If he left the ship, anyone could put a man on the vessel and claim it. 'It was my duty to take my ship around the world. It would have been morally wrong to leave,' he later said. As sixty-foot waves battered the ship over the next fifteen days, Carlsen used a makeshift radio to maintain contact with other ships nearby, and he scavenged for food and water on the sinking craft. Finally, after all attempts to rescue the vessel failed, the captain jumped from the listing ship and swam to safety.

Captain Carlsen was surprised to find cheering crowds waiting for him at the port in Falmouth. He was cheered as a hero then and on many subsequent occasions. He just could not appreciate why. After all, he had merely done his duty.

He was offered $250,000 by the *Daily Express* for an exclusive story. He was approached by Hollywood with a $500,000 offer for a film. He turned both down. 'I do not want a seaman's honest attempt to save his ship used for any commercial purpose,' he said. The only offer he accepted was the chance to captain *Flying Enterprise II*.

In an interview many decades later, a journalist asked Captain Carlsen what lesson he had learned from the experience. 'To do what you are supposed to do,' was his reply.

Bewildering and complex world

The dictionary definition of 'authentic' is 'conforming to fact and therefore worthy of trust, reliance or belief'. Its synonyms are listed as bona fide, genuine, real, and undoubted. There really is not much difference between the dictionary definition and the popular understanding.

The world and society have both become bewildering and complex. Presidents and prime ministers of almost every nation on the planet seem to have lost their marbles. Chief executives of several famous companies are buffeted by serious credibility issues: GlaxoSmithKline for improper marketing, the Royal Bank of Scotland for goofing up customer accounts and Barclays for fixing interest rates, among others. I should not forget India's examples, with 2G, land leases, coal and iron ore mines. All these examples raise questions about the authenticity of leaders.

Professor Ibarra states that there are three reasons why leaders struggle with authenticity. First, people make more frequent and basic changes in the work they do, and such changes require change. Second, business is often conducted across borders, forcing people to work with culturally diverse colleagues and partners. Third, leaders are always being watched, what with hierarchy, ubiquitous connectivity and social media.

Just about anybody you can think of considers the word authenticity in a way that is similar to the dictionary definition. If this is the meaning, is it a virtue to be authentic when applied to human relations? Perhaps not. Life would be impossible if every person said or did what is really on his or her mind. According to Clancy Martin, professor of philosophy at the University of

Missouri, Kansas City, we all tell lies, and tell them shockingly often ('Good lovers lie,' Clancy Martin, *International Herald Tribune*, February 8, 2015). 'When it comes to love, both honesty and deception should be practised in moderation,' wrote Martin. 'Only then can we celebrate the intoxicating illusions of love... Love is a greater good than truth.'

The harsh truth is that you would make an awful spouse if you were to share every thought or opinion exactly as you think or feel. It would be the same between a boss and a subordinate. In no human relationship can you communicate exactly what you feel. Does that make you unauthentic? You would not agree with such an assessment.

We associate authenticity with sincerity, honesty and integrity. We assume that it is an innate quality in every human being: that each individual is authentic or is not. We assume that an authentic person is consistently so and, conversely, unauthentic people are always so. Authenticity is thought of as the opposite of artifice, which means not straightforward and sincere.

This way of thinking about authenticity is flawed, and is just not true. The reality is that your behaviour is a planned balance between expressing your personality and managing the impressions of those whom you wish to relate with. Yes, managing others, but that does not have to connote manipulation or untruthfulness. The yawning gap between the general imagery and the practice of authenticity spawns questions about behavioural ethics.

If you have had a bad experience with a person, you think of that person as unreliable and unauthentic. If someone else has had a good experience with the same person, he or she thinks in the opposite way to you. The person is the same but the circumstances of the relationship determine whether or not the person is regarded as authentic or not.

A person who is perceived in the workplace as an authentic manager may be one who is cheating on his wife. An authentic and dutiful son may behave deceitfully to achieve a particular goal. The great Sri Rama, in the epic Ramayana, is held as the epitome of human character and authenticity. However, there is one episode in which he, the incarnation of Lord Vishnu, hides behind a tree and kills his enemy, Vali, to help his ally, Sugreeva. Virtuous men do not hide behind trees and attack!

How we think of authenticity

What then is authenticity and who is authentic? I rather like what Stephen Covey wrote: that when you behave exactly as your dog would expect you to, it is authenticity! Since I am not a dog adulating person, let me explain in human terms. Through my experiences, I have concluded that certain aspects of authenticity that are really worthwhile to remember.

Authentic people are quick to admit when they have screwed up. It may be at work or it may be in a personal relationship. They confront the reality, accept their mistake and get right out to do what is necessary. Authentic people are comfortable with themselves and where they come from. They always remember who they are.

But what is authenticity, and can you take too literally the advice to just be yourself. Whether you are a subordinate or a boss, husband or wife, landlord or tenant, you would consider it a virtue to be perceived as authentic. You have to learn how to manage your authenticity. Authentic people must have the chameleon's ability to adapt to different situations. Authenticity is not the same as manipulation. You must learn which personality traits you have to reveal and to whom, depending on what is appropriate. I knew a senior leader who had become a bit stern and distant as he rose in the organisation. On his appointment to the pinnacle as managing director, his earliest buddies and colleagues hosted a private dinner party for him, where I was also invited.

The managing director was a different man, laughing, cracking jokes and just enjoying himself by being himself. I admired the manner in which he managed his authenticity.

Authenticity means learning from the muddle of real life. We have created a utopian imagery in which we dream that we should have fewer and fewer problems as we rise. We yearn for increasing certainty. The reality of life and career is exactly the opposite. You are paid your salary to swim with alligators in a swirling river and still come out winning. You have to be immersed in your work and continuously learn from the muddles of uncertainty, ambiguity and real-life problems. These are the experiences that make a person authentic.

Authenticity comes from common sense and self-awareness. Authentic people become authentic through experiences and not necessarily through deep meditational techniques or psychobabble. Personally I am a bit wary of 'authenticity consultants' (yes, they exist; just Google the words). To me authenticity consulting smacks of a lack of authenticity. In my simple way of thinking, the apostles of authenticity are not too far away from the masters of intrigue.

Authenticity is connected with deep personal and professional relationships. You can identify an authentic person when you interact with one. You can, equally, spot an unauthentic person when you see one. The vast majority of people you meet will be neither very authentic nor very unauthentic. In fact, you will regard as authentic those people with whom you have a great relationship. You judge the authenticity through your relationship.

Authentic people do what they have to because that is what they simply have to do. Given a difficult circumstance, people will act in a way which truly represents who they are. They are not influenced by the after effects of their actions or their image of authenticity.

When I was a departmental head, I discovered a fraud in my

department. After some confusion in my mind, I went straight up to my chief executive and told him that I was in trouble. The whole company rallied to rescue me from my predicament. On another occasion, when I ran the animal feeds division, there were some bird deaths due to the feed being consumed by the birds. I was incensed with my plant-in-charge, who confirmed to the regulator that one of the grinders in the plant was malfunctioning and that the bird deaths may have occurred due to the birds consuming the company's feed. I insisted on sacking that plant-in-charge. In his mind he was being authentic. In my mind I will never know whether I did the right thing by asking for his resignation.

Dilemmas of life—the story of Venu

I learnt the story of a friend called Venu. Venu ended with a roundabout resolution to an exasperating problem that should never have occurred. Venu worked in the Indian subsidiary of a multinational company. There was a difference of opinion between Venu and the Securities Exchange Board of India (SEBI) with regard to some share transaction done by Venu. The episode taught Venu (and me) a few lessons about truth and authenticity, and that is why the episode finds a place here. When you finish reading this story, try answering whether Venu had an authentic response to the challenge he faced.

When Venu went overseas for a four-year posting in the 1990s, he could save a little money for the first time in his life. He also became familiar with the 'flavour of those times': increasing employee engagement and commitment through equity participation. When he returned to head his company, these ideas were fresh in his mind.

Upon return he found that his company had more problems than he had anticipated. Its stock price was depressed. He was reasonably certain that the situation could be turned around if the motivation of the embattled managers could be shored up and they could continue to be assured of their future. He thought one appropriate way was to demonstrate his confidence in his plans was to place some of his personal savings at risk by buying the company's stock from the market at prevailing prices.

He asked the legal director and the company chairman whether the company had any rules pertaining to senior managers buying shares in the open market. The corporate governance environment was very different from today and explicit rules on these kinds of subjects were not always explicit in those days. The legal director and chairman set out the procedures to be followed.

In line with that document, Venu sought the board's permission to invest in a certain number of shares. A formal letter was received by Venu, permitting him to buy the shares within a specified window of time, which were the few weeks between the announcements of the company's two successive quarterly results, called an open period.

He did so and upon completion of the market transaction, Venu reported back to the board. At the next board meeting, the purchase was noted by the board as a transaction having been done within the rules. So far as he was concerned, that was the end of the matter. He had no intention to trade in those shares anyway.

The SEBI investigation began based on some information that SEBI had gathered. During the session with Venu, the officers asked whether he owned any shares. Naturally, he disclosed that he had bought personal shares as per the company procedures and with full disclosure over nine months prior to the period which was engaging SEBI's attention. His disclosure was taken on record.

To Venu's great surprise, a report appeared in the press that SEBI was to investigate his transactions. Without his having received any letter of investigation, the issue was on the front pages of newspapers one morning. Comments began to be written in the press. Venu felt deeply hurt and aggrieved that such a thing should have happened. For the next four years, the matter was neither pursued nor resolved by SEBI. Not a single letter was written to Venu, nor was he asked any questions.

Venu voluntarily called on the SEBI officials concerned to request that the matter be disposed of, whatever the outcome. He told them that the only capital he had acquired after thirty years of corporate work was the reputation of professionalism and integrity, and he felt that this capital should not be placed at risk by procrastination or deliberate delays.

After this meeting Venu was verbally told that, in fact, there was no personal case at all. SEBI officials were concerned, it seemed, that a closure of his case could appear in the media. The officers said that they were sensitive to this.

Venu thought to himself, 'What about my sensitivity?'

Finally, after he had gone through four years of mental agony, Venu got a telephone call from a senior SEBI officer. 'We have just signed a twelve-page order closing your personal case; it is over,' he said. 'Please, can you collect the order from our office?'

'Well, thank you. It is now an old matter, so why do you not send it to me by post?' Venu asked him. The officer appeared reluctant to do so for some reason. As a matter of principle, and quite logically, Venu was inclined to decline the suggestion to collect the order from the SEBI office. Instinctively, however, he decided that such a case could be more damaging if left unresolved. For the next many years that it would take to resolve the matter, in things such as passport applications and board disclosures, he might need to answer in the affirmative a question like, 'Is there any case pending against you?' Why should he carry the burden of something like that?

So Venu sent his driver to collect it. This narrative, coming as it does after many years caused Venu a great deal of mental turmoil and personal anguish. He felt deeply victimised by an unfair system.

He learnt three instructive lessons from this, all pointing to different lens-eye views.

Firstly, he was viewing this matter as a personal case, but SEBI had reframed the issue and viewed it within its larger surveillance context. Naturally Venu thought that was unfair, but there it was. Secondly, to Venu it was a non-case and there was no ambiguity at all. SEBI concurred informally but found a circuitous route to reach that conclusion, for reasons that appear mysterious and illogical. SEBI was under pressure in those days for being ineffective. In pursuing the case, it must have had mixed motives, based on its own agenda of those times. Thirdly, Venu thought it was a matter of principle not to accept delivery at the SEBI office. He hesitated. But then, intuitively, he felt the need to compromise by not letting the matter lie unresolved. He could not afford to be a hero on this relatively minor matter; he needed to be practical. If he had not found it possible to compromise, it could still be an unresolved case—and only he would be the aggrieved and unhappy, and not anybody in SEBI.

Is there a compass that can guide us on how to deal with such ambiguous situations effectively? Yes, honesty of purpose, values. And acting authentically. Those are the companions of the person who tries to find an effective way out of a problem. They help him be himself, and do things naturally.

Spiral of silence

Most of us are aware of Lord Browne, the iconic group chief executive officer of British Petroleum (BP) who undertook a spectacular and inspiring journey, from being an apprentice at the company in 1966 to becoming one of the most celebrated business icons in the world. This incredible journey saw him being credited with revamping BP's profile within the petroleum industry, reducing overheads by cutting down the workforce and improving efficiencies, acquiring major natural resource companies and, in the process, making BP one of the largest and most profitable companies in the world.

Knighted by Queen Elizabeth in 1998—and also dubbed Lord Browne of Madingley in 2001—he was showered with numerous accolades, from the United Nations to the Royal Academy of Engineering, besides being voted Britain's most admired chief executive by *Management Today* for three consecutive years from 2000 to 2002.

In 2007, in bizarre turn of events, Lord Browne was unceremoniously asked to quit BP.

What could have caused this sudden fall from grace?

On the surface it may seem that it was the public revelation of his sexual preferences and his embarrassment at lying to the court about his relationship with his boyfriend that led him to put in his papers in May 2007. If we peel the layers and go to the core, certain facts emerge that establish that the seeds of his departure were sown much earlier.

Even before the news of his quitting BP was made public, the board, then led by Peter Sutherland, had already forced Lord Browne to announce that he would retire by the end of 2008. This, after a series of operational disasters at BP under Browne's watch, including an explosion at the company's Texas oil refinery and a large oil spill in Alaska. These were serious accidents, leading to 15 deaths and 170 injuries in Texas and an estimated 267,000 gallons of oil leaking from BP's pipelines in Alaska. The Alaska spill led to a criminal investigation and the discovery that miles of BP's pipeline were dangerously corroded.

When disasters like these happen despite such an iconic leader at the helm, one is compelled to ask, 'Were these accidents only a symptom of a larger problem attributed to the leadership style that the big bosses at BP wanted to address by expediting Lord

Browne's ouster?'

To answer this, we perhaps need to delve into Lord Browne's leadership style and understand how it could have affected the actions and behaviour of his team.

Lord Browne had become a business icon, was rubbing shoulders with statesmen and world leaders, and the media had been gushing in its praise for him and in handing him fancy sobriquets. As is the case with most people, it must have been difficult for Lord Browne to stay grounded and not be blinded by this glory. When everybody is calling you a visionary, it gives you good reason to conveniently rely only on your judgment and not pay heed to what others think. Lord Browne has suggested in his memoirs that his arrogance and a culture of complacency contributed to BP's failure to prevent the Alaska oil spill.

'As a leader it is hard to find that delicate balance between confidence, humility and arrogance,' admitted Lord Browne. 'You need confidence to make decisions to keep moving the business forward...yet arrogance may cause you to make a decision before considering the range of possibilities.' Was it possible that success made him arrogant to the extent that he was not welcoming or, rather, was dismissive of others' views? Did his behaviour discourage his people from questioning his decisions? Tony Howard, who succeeded Lord Browne, sort of summed this up in December 2006: 'We have a leadership style that is too directive and doesn't listen sufficiently well. The top of the organisation doesn't listen sufficiently to what the bottom is saying.'

Andrew Grove of Intel remembers how, when Lord Browne spoke at a meeting, everyone would become quite and listen intently. Lord Browne was tough, cerebral and a workaholic who frightened subordinates with his calm, penetrating assessments of their work. It is said that monthly meetings were sessions during which he grilled managers on every aspect of their work. Those who produced positive results were rewarded with challenging projects and promotions; those who did not were asked to leave. There might be a possibility that his intolerance of shortcomings was making his subordinates reluctant to confront him even on issues of importance.

Lord Browne was not known to be emotional or compassionate. His leadership style comes across as being directive, authoritative, and intolerant of failure, one that discouraged any freeway communication, one that led to creation of a big spiral of silence.

This is what probably went against Lord Browne and BP. The spiral of silence prevented even matters of the greatest significance from reaching Lord Browne. 'I wish someone had challenged me and been brave enough to say: "we need to ask more disagreeable questions."' he is said to have said after the Alaska oil spill. The spiral had reached a proportion where it was threatening BPs image and existence. The board may have had no other option but to usher in change that would make the work environment at BP more transparent.

In general, across any setup there is a huge cost associated with the spiral of silence. These spirals multiply across all levels once they get formed at the top, and soon infect the entire organisation. Important information is withheld, information that can impact the quality of work of employees and organisations. When employees stay silent, they keep new ideas to themselves and leave alternative courses of action unexplored. Scandals at Enron, Tyco and WorldCom, to name a few, show how catastrophic situations can become when silence prevails. Behind failed products, broken processes and mistaken decisions are people who chose to hold their tongues rather than speak up.

Everybody concerned has a role in breaking the spiral, including leaders and employees, because this affects everybody. Keeping quiet is too big a problem to be just left to leaders. Having said that, the problem gets compounded for iconic leaders like Lord Browne since their stature and larger-than-life image creates a great power expanse between subordinates and themselves. This distance reduces the scope of different opinions reaching leaders. Consequently, there is the critical need for leaders to be willing to take the first step to bring differences out in the open so that they can be explored. They need to reach out to others to break the hold of silence.

Breaking the silence would mean unleashing the flow of fresh ideas, leading to the outpouring of constructive viewpoints and brilliant thoughts that have the potential to take organisations to the next level.

Authenticity has no mantra

All of these examples illustrate that nobody can be authentic to all people at all times on all issues. There is no concept of what I might call universal authenticity.

The first essential quality of a leader is to be just who he is; above all, he or she must not try to be different things to different people. As Ratan Tata often said when he succeeded JRD Tata, he decided to be himself instead of emulating JRD Tata or thinking of how JRD would have approached a problem.

The second essential quality is to understand one's own weaknesses. There is no point concealing weaknesses, as everybody has some. Ratan Tata admitted openly that as a person he is somewhat private and publicity shy. He was who he was, and he conducted his affairs in that way.

The third aspect is that the self transforms, not through born leadership traits but by being 'baked and cooked in the crucibles of experience'. Ratan Tata has recounted many times how his leadership and approaches were shaped by, for example, the tough union situation he encountered at the Pune plant of TELCO in the late 1980s.

The fourth aspect is that one cannot lead authentically without compassion. In people-related matters, one cannot be harsh or wall oneself away from those affected. Jamshed Irani's narrations in chapter 11 about his experiences after the Jamshedpur fire on March 3, 1989, and about the reduction of the workforce in TISCO in the mid-1990s both illustrate this.

Before I joined the Tata group, I had learnt that in any extrovert business crowd, one might not even notice Ratan Tata's presence because he is so low profile and self-effacing. That he is. But, amazingly, there are some people you notice precisely for that. I wish to focus on just one of his many attributes. It is the attribute of courage, which leaps out in discussions with him, irrespective of whether you agree or disagree with his point of view.

An episode occurred in April 2001 and so far as I know, the matter is still sub judice. It was approaching midnight and I was at a dinner party when my cell phone rang. A journalist was on the line, tipping me off about an anonymous letter doing the media rounds and referring to some wrongdoings at Tata Finance. Though it was late, I called Vice-Chairman Noshir Soonawala. He had already been woken up by another caller.

Over the next few days, a letter dated April 12, 2001, reached the desks of several senior Tata leaders, purportedly from one Shankar Sharma (the real name is still not known). The letter levelled serious allegations against the Tata Finance's serving managing director Dilip Pendse. It alleged that a fraud had been committed in the company. There was a sense of shock and disbelief among the recipients. In my experience, in such a situation it happens often that an embarrassed company leadership tries hard to suppress the facts, gloss over the details and work desperately to keep the matter out of the media.

Ratan Tata did exactly the opposite.

The full story of what happened thence has been told in two publications: in an article entitled 'Grime and salvation' in the Tata group's house magazine as well as in a book, *Tata Log* (New Delhi, 2012), written by Harish Bhat.

Tata leaders like Noshir Soonawala, Ishaat Hussain and Bharat Vasani were quickly assembled by Ratan Tata. Their mandate was to study the matter and deal with the issues with total openness. Their team had his active guidance. Ratan Tata had defined two clear principles: first, the interests of every depositor would be fully protected so that no one who had trusted the Tata name lost; second, a thorough investigation would be completed so that the guilty could be legally pursued and punished.

It must be remembered that Tata Sons could have merely adhered to its limited legal responsibilities, rather than meet 100 per cent of the financial liabilities of a company which was not owned 100 per cent by Tata. In the early days the nature and extent of the damage were both fuzzy and extremely worrying. During this period there was a Tata Chemicals annual general meeting of shareholders.

Although Tata Finance was not an appropriate subject for this meeting, some elderly shareholders wailed with great emotion that they may lose their limited savings in Tata Finance. To my astonishment, Ratan Tata stood up and boldly announced that Tata would stand behind every small investor. Nobody needs to fear losing his or her valuable and hard-earned savings. I was stunned that a business leader could be so empathetic and make such a public commitment. He instinctively acted on the principle that when there is a crisis you just have to do what your sense of duty and conscience dictates.

The episode illustrated the behaviour of a courageous leader who cared deeply about responsible leadership and humanism. It was a rare cocktail.

8

Courage: The Third Lens

'To see what is right, and not to do it, is want of courage or of principle.'

—Confucius

'Our greatest glory is not in never failing, but in rising up every time we fail.'

—Ralph Waldo Emerson

Almost everyone is fascinated by courage, even though very few are able to define what it is. When we hear about someone who has performed a physically courageous task like conquering Mount Everest, performing a daring act in war, dealing upfront with an ethical issue, or upholding a deeply felt belief, we admire the act. For what? For the act of courage.

Courage is like beauty—one cannot quite describe it, but we recognise it when it appears. We endeavour to face up to the moments of truth that arise in our own lives, to beat the odds, and live a life full of courage. Courage is about displays of ambition, boldness, standing up for the weak, taking risk and facing up to one's vulnerabilities.

But we need to understand the word courage a little more intimately. History provides examples of courage in every country.

History is the historian's impression of what happened, based on the facts gathered, what he or she has been able to interpret and as viewed through that person's eyes. Leaders are portrayed to be courageous in battle and administration. Some like Akbar and Shivaji are unequivocally placed on a pedestal, and some others like Aurangzeb, are a bit controversial.

Ushering in change is a big management subject. Managers are deeply interested in the subject of change management in organisations because while the technical aspects of change are not difficult to assess, the human aspects of change can be ambiguous and frustrating.

I narrate a six hundred year story from Korean history on the subject of ushering in change in social thinking among a tradition-bound population.

King Sejong

King Sejong ruled Korea from 1418. In a book on courage, Sejong's story has been cited as an example of courage to change a status quo (Merom Klein and Rod Napier, *The Courage to Act*, Palo Alto, 2003).

Sejong the Great became monarch of Korea when he was twenty-two and ruled for thirty-two years till 1450. At the end of his reign, he had transformed Korea from a country with a low literacy level to a nation with one of the highest literacy levels in Asia. How did he balance his lofty vision with the travails of execution?

Sejong inherited a Korea with abysmal literacy levels. He had a moment of truth when he decided to transform the situation. His rule was absolute and he had the power to force change on his feudal society. However, lasting change does not happen by forcing. He imagined what Korea could be with education, prosperity and empowerment. He had to identify the bottlenecks.

During Sejong's rule, since there was no Korean alphabet, the educated elite used Chinese characters for writing. The result was that the spoken Korean and the written Korean had divergences. Sejong decided to invent a new Korean alphabet, which he called Hangeul. The elite would not accept the Hangeul alphabet (they had always used the Chinese alphabet) and the illiterate would not welcome it because learning any alphabet was a nuisance.

Sejong decided to move around incognito among his people to learn first-hand what they thought about Hangeul. Armed with direct feedback about issues and problems, he adapted Hangeul suitably. When the new alphabet was resisted by the elite and the common people, Sejong had the letters etched on the barks of trees to give people the impression that it was the will of God. A purist could consider this to be an act of misusing trust by playing on the people's ignorance and gullibility. A shift of the lens through which the act is viewed can show it as an act of courage.

His advisors were concerned about the social turmoil among the educated population, but Sejong embraced even wider forms of social and economic reforms to accelerate the emancipation of his people. 'The tremendous opportunity for progress is worth the risk,' he seemed to think.

Klein and Napier have developed a model of five courage factors. Using the example of King Sejong, the authors have pointed out how he displayed all these courage factors through the work that he dedicated his life to. According to them, courage has five constituents:

- First is *candour* (the courage to speak and hear the truth).
- Second is *purpose* (the courage to pursue lofty and audacious goals).
- Third is *will* (the courage to inspire optimism).
- Fourth is *rigour* (the courage to invent discipline and make it stick).
- Fifth and last is *risk* (the courage to invest in relationships).

King Sejong's story demonstrates that in the display of courage, the view through another lens can be different. This was so with the Sejong's messages on the barks of the trees. But if that is what is necessary to accomplish the task, then courageous leaders do so.

The yardsticks to judge acts of courage are not universal. To adapt Leo Tolstoy's opening lines from *Anna Karenina*, all successful courage stories are similar, but every unsuccessful courage story fails for its own reason. Who is to judge what courage is and what the yardsticks are?

How you judge courage

Subhas Chandra Bose fought hard against the British colonialists from the 1920s onwards. He undertook daring acts of defiance to challenge the British rulers of India. People of my age grew up on a diet of his courage. The British rulers, however, thought of Bose differently, seeing him as a subversive revolutionary who had teamed up with their enemies (the Germans and the Japanese) during a catastrophic war.

What constitutes success in a courage narrative? Is it only the upholding of the principle one fights for? Or does the courage have something to do with the outcome of the challenge? Or is it the retention of the status and position from which one expresses the disagreement?

The subject is made further complex by the fact that a person who demonstrates courage in one situation may not display it in another?

I have found it helpful to think of courage in human terms—acting in line with your deeply held beliefs about what is right and wrong. My point is illustrated by the example of A.P. Venkateshwaran (or APV for short), a distinguished member of the Indian Foreign Service (IFS). He died in 2014 at the age of eighty-five.

APV was a blunt, no-nonsense officer who served thirty-five years in the IFS before becoming being eligible for appointment, in 1986, as India's foreign secretary. Rajiv Gandhi was the prime minister then. APV was the senior-most in line to become the foreign secretary, he began hearing through the grapevine that he may be sent as ambassador to Soviet Union to make place for his junior to be appointed to the post.

APV asked to see the prime minister. He told him that he had not come to lobby for the foreign secretary post, but merely to request that if he were to be bypassed for the job, he would rather retire prematurely. Rajiv Gandhi called APV two days later. He communicated that APV would indeed be the next foreign secretary and said, 'Let's have bash at it.' Such a comment can be considered ungracious when applied to a foreign secretary who had put in such long service.

From the start APV had the dice loaded against him. *India Today* magazine said he was 'a renaissance man capable of quoting from Emerson and the Upanishads in the same breath and does not suffer fools or manipulative politicians gladly'. Further, he had registered his strong objections to the manner in which India was bending over backwards to appease Sri Lanka on the Tamils issue. He had also objected to the exclusion of the foreign office in the talks with Pakistan on the Siachen dispute.

Rajiv Gandhi was an inexperienced prime minister. One of his weaknesses was that 'he would get impressed by presentations that contained modern gadgets, slides and graphs', according to his cabinet secretary, B.G. Deshmukh. (*A Cabinet Secretary Looks Back,* New Delhi, 2004). Rajiv Gandhi was 'a bit impatient and often tempted to ride roughshod over old-fashioned civil servants…he was more inclined towards suave advisors who came from public schools…'

Gradually Rajiv Gandhi was persuaded by his coterie of advisors that APV had the habit of exceeding his brief. One instance pertained to his statement that the prime minister had agreed to visit Pakistan. Another instance was his statement that Sri Lanka had hired American mercenaries to battle the Tamil militants. Rajiv Gandhi was furious. APV seemed all set to become a tragic victim of the powerbrokers around the prime minister.

In an unplanned, and therefore unexpected, announcement at a press conference, Rajiv Gandhi stated that soon the journalists would be 'talking to a new foreign secretary'. Everybody, literally everyone, was left dumbfounded. It reflected very poorly on the prime minister. APV promptly resigned. It took some effort on the part of Deshmukh, to persuade him to seek premature retirement so that he could have the terminal benefits of retirement. APV went away quietly into retirement in Bangalore.

Was APV courageous? He lost his position, but he upheld his principles. Is it inevitable that when you uphold principles you end up losing personally?

Courage is a very wide term. It can be applied to acts of valour and heroism, like to the captain of a ship who gives up his life to save his passengers. It can be applied to war when a soldier sacrifices his life in defence of the country. It can be applied to a pedestrian who goes out of his or her way to save a road accident victim. The list is endless.

Leadership courage

For the purpose of this chapter, the word will be restricted to leadership courage: in the face of one prevalent view in an unfavourable atmosphere, how can an opposing view be expressed? This is a common situation in leadership when one is required to speak one's mind.

A person may express differences against a prevalent view among seniors because of four underlying reasons:

- Difference of opinion (I disagree with your opinion).
- Assertion of ego (I am right and I would not like to be seen to be yielding to your view).
- Matter of principle (I am unable to support this on the basis of a non-financial principle).
- Question of ethics (I don't support it because there seems to be financial wrongdoing).

A study of mythology, history and business is interesting and instructive. In each of the five courage cases written below, there is a difference of opinion between a subordinate and a superior, and they have some sort of a hierarchical relationship. The driver for the difference ranges from a simple opinion or point of view up to one involving financial impropriety. It is instructive to judge each of these cases of courage for the issue, its driver and the outcome.

General Bucher and Vallabhbhai Patel: A different opinion on Hyderabad police action

The following story demonstrates the courage of General Bucher is speaking up at the right time and in accepting a different decision from his recommendation.

India became independent on August 15, 1947. Those were tumultuous times for the nation. Right after independence, Kashmir suffered infiltration from across the new border with Pakistan. A war between India and Pakistan over Kashmir began on October 22, 1947. At about the same time, problems brewed in the princely state of Hyderabad. Events unfolded simultaneously in Kashmir and Hyderabad.

The state of Hyderabad is located over most of India's Deccan plateau. The dynasty and kingdom was established in 1724 by Asaf Jah after the collapse of the Moghul Empire. By the time of independence, Hyderabad was the largest in area among all the 565 princely states of India, and the wealthiest by far. It had its own army, airline, telecommunications network, railways, postal system, radio broadcasting service and currency. Hyderabad's ruler was the Nizam, a Muslim, while a majority of the subject population was Hindu (85 per cent were Hindu and 12 per cent Muslim as per the 1941 census).

Since the beginning of the twentieth century, the state had started to become increasingly theocratic. In 1926, a retired Hyderabad official, Mahmud Nawaz Khan, founded the *Ittehad* (also known as MIM). Its objective was 'to unite the Muslims in the State in support of the Nizam and to reduce the Hindu majority by large-scale conversion to Islam'. *Ittehad* emerged as a powerful communal organization, one that marginalised the political aspirations of the Hindu and the moderate Muslim population. It is from this organisation that Qasim Razwi emerged when the Nizam felt threatened by the events surrounding Indian independence. With the Nizam's tacit approval, Qasim Razvi put together a volunteer militia of Muslims; this came to be known as the Razakars.

In 1947, when Patel approached Hyderabad to sign the instrument of accession, the Nizam refused. He declared Hyderabad an independent state even though it was located in the heart of India. When Patel requested the help of the English governor general, Lord Mountbatten, he was advised to resolve the issue without the use of force. Accordingly, the Indian Government offered Hyderabad a 'Standstill Agreement', which assured that the status quo would be maintained and negotiations could continue. Lord Mountbatten himself presided over the negotiations and several possible deals were developed, but were all rejected by the Hyderabad government.

There was considerable turmoil and unrest developing in Hyderabad right after independence. On December 4, 1947, a Hindu leader, Narayan Rao Pawar, made a failed attempt to assassinate the Nizam. The Nizam had nurtured a large army, with mercenaries hired from among Arabs, Rohillas and Pathans. The army was commanded by an Arab, Major General Zain El Edroos. Even as India and Hyderabad negotiated through 1948, the Nizam tacitly encouraged the Razakars to escalate the violence between them and the Hindu community. Qasim Razwi made inflammatory statements openly, such as, 'We will see that no Razakar steps into India, but if a single soldier of yours steps into our territory, 500,000 Razakars will march into India, and I cannot say where they will stop.'

By March 1948, Lord Mountbatten heard rumours of an Indian plan called Operation Polo to move Indian troops into Hyderabad. He sent for the British commander-in-chief of the Indian Army, General Roy Bucher, to enquire what Polo was about. Bucher stated that he knew nothing about it. Later, after an enquiry, he clarified that it was the Indian Government's contingency plan should a massacre of Hindus occur in Hyderabad.

In June 1948, Lord Mountbatten prepared the 'heads of agreement' deal, which offered Hyderabad the status of an autonomous dominion nation under India. The deal called for the restriction of the regular Hyderabad armed forces along with the disbanding of the militant Razakars. The Nizam would continue to be the executive head of the state pending a plebiscite and elections. This plan, too, was rejected by the Nizam. Let alone signing an agreement, the Nizam issued a *firman* on June 12 demanding complete independence from India.

Patel was progressively getting tired of the Nizam's actions and wanted to put a quick end to the deteriorating string of developments. Patel wondered, 'How can the belly breathe if it is cut off from the main body?' The civil law and order situation in Hyderabad was deteriorating fast thanks to the activities of the Razakars. Patel told Lord Mountbatten, 'The Nizam has mortgaged his future to his own Frankenstein, the *Ittehad*.'

Patel summoned Maj. Gen. Chaudhuri, the army chief in southern India, to assess his confidence and preparedness if the plans to enter Hyderabad were to be implemented. It was V.K. Krishna Menon, the Indian high commissioner in London, who suggested the terminology 'police action' rather than army action, even though it was clearly an army action. For such a plan to be implemented, cabinet sanction was essential. Jawaharlal Nehru was most reluctant and Patel actually walked out of one cabinet meeting in protest. Nehru was jolted out of his complacency and started to relent. But he was under the contrary influence of Bucher, who was hesitant throughout the planning. Bucher overestimated the capacity of the Hyderabad army and underestimated that of his own troops.

A cabinet meeting was organised on September 12, 1948, to take a final decision. Among those who attended were Nehru, Patel, Baldev Singh, the defence minister, General Bucher, Air Force chief Air Marshall Sir Thomas Elmhurst and Lt Gen. KM Cariappa. As the decision to begin the Hyderabad police action got crystallised, General Bucher stood up and said, 'Gentlemen, you have taken a decision in a difficult matter. I must give you my warning. We are also committed in Kashmir. We cannot say how long it will take, so we will end up having two operations on our hands. This is not advisable, so as your commander in chief I ask you not to start the operations.'

It was an act of great courage that the general spoke up clearly when it was required. General Bucher offered his resignation if his advice was not heeded. There was a silence while a distressed and worried Nehru looked around. Patel interjected at this pont: 'You may resign, General Bucher, but the police action will start tomorrow.' A disappointed General Bucher left the room. The Hyderabad police action began the next day, on September 13. Within five days the Nizam's forces were routed. By 4 pm on

September 17, Maj. Gen. Zain El Edroos surrendered to the Indian Army's Maj. Gen. J.N. Chaudhuri in Secunderabad.

The leaders in India and Pakistan were both new to their national roles and somewhat inexperienced. The last thing either of them could afford was a war, but the two leaderships must have felt the pressure to demonstrate that they were in charge.

The British had left in a technical sense, but not quite in reality. Independent first governor general was Lord Mountbatten and the commanders in chief of both armies were British nationals. The few remaining British officials must have had good channels of communication between themselves and certainly great averseness to a war as they were about to depart. Patel was a pragmatic leader who viewed the Hyderabad situation with great concern. Being a person with planning as a strength, Patel must have worked out alternatives and contingencies. By September 1948, Patel was really impatient with the intransigence of the Nizam and started insisting that Operation Polo begin soon.

General Bucher was fifty-three years of age at the time of these events and probably looking forward to retiring from India and returning to his home country, which he did in early 1949. He had shown some signs of being an inflexible officer at the time of independence, when he passed an order that the 'public be kept away from flag hoisting'. Nehru had to rescind that order and remind the general of the Indian Government's supremacy.

General Bucher was at best hesitant, if not always opposed, to any army action in Hyderabad. For him the disagreement was not a matter of ethics or principle; it was one of judgment on whether the nascent army could handle two difficult situations simultaneously. He probably had much to lose by supporting the police action, but little to lose by opposing it since his retirement was imminent.

When Patel took a firm line, General Bucher did not do any drama or resign; in fact he ensured that the valid instructions (taken by the right people after listening to alternate views) to be fully implemented. Though opposed to war, he was deeply conscious of the unreasonableness of the Nizam, as evidenced by his letter to his daughter six months before the police action. 'The real trouble in Hyderabad seems to be that the Nizam has become bound hand and foot to the *Ittehad*,' he wrote. 'The Indian policy is one of reasonableness insofar as this is possible.'

Patel was very gracious towards General Bucher. After the successful Operation Polo, Patel wrote a letter of congratulation to him: 'I should like to send you and your officers and the men under their command my sincerest felicitations on the successful completion of the Hyderabad operations...'

Vibhishana and Ravana—a case of a non-financial principle

In the great Indian epic the Ramayana, there is a character called Ravana. He is popularly depicted as a demon with ten heads. He is the 'bad guy' of the story, the one who abducts the wife (Sita) of the hero of the story (Rama). A monkey god called Hanuman plays the key role in finding where the abducted Sita has been incarcerated. He delivered Rama's message of solace to her and returned safely back to Rama to report about the whereabouts of his abducted wife.

Although Ravana is depicted throughout the story in a bad light, his scholarly and spiritual accomplishments were outstanding. He was the son of a learned sage, who, in turn, was the son of a renowned sage. Ravana's father and grandfather had imparted to him a tremendously distinguished lineage. Among his siblings, he had a brother by the name of Vibhishana, who is relevant to this story because he comes through as wise and patient.

His father had noticed as he grew up that Ravana was aggressive and arrogant, but also that he was an exemplary scholar.

He mastered the Vedas and other holy books. He was a master at playing the musical instrument, the veena. Ravana also undertook severe austerities and won boons from the gods.

His positive accomplishments aside, Ravana had performed a very, very evil deed in abducting Sita. He carried her away forcibly to his land, Lanka. She was incarcerated and hidden in a forest and given two months to voluntarily agree to marry Ravana.

With great heroism and after overcoming many obstacles, Hanuman, acting as Rama's emissary, managed to find Sita in Lanka. He wins her trust, conveys to her a message of hope from her husband, and gets prepared to return to Rama with a positive and reassuring message of her safety from her.

Before returning from Lanka, Hanuman considered it important to meet Ravana and deliver him a warning. He wanted to tell him that war could still be avoided if he admitted his error and graciously returned Sita to her husband. But how was Hanuman to penetrate the security system around Ravana and get an audition to deliver his message?

Hanuman went on the rampage in Lanka, burning palaces and destroying warriors. He figured that in this way the troops and army would be sent after him to arrest him. He could choose a convenient timing during these arrest proceedings to allow himself to be overcome. His captors would proudly present him to Ravana. In this way Hanuman could penetrate the tight security at the palace of the mighty king and deliver his message.

This was the precise plan of action that Hanuman implemented. After the destruction of the gardens and the palaces and the killing of Ravana's generals, Lanka was in considerable panic. Hanuman allowed himself to be bound in ropes and dragged along to the terrified court within the palace of Ravana.

When he saw the palace, Hanuman was hugely impressed. In fact, he felt daunted. It was a majestic palace and Ravana was arraigned in expensive clothes with jewellery. Very accomplished and well-known ministers, administrators and generals sat in the full court of the king. Ministers and generals were assigned the task of questioning Hanuman to understand who he was, why he had come to Lanka and under what provocation he had committed all the heinous crimes of destruction.

It was a tense atmosphere. Ravana was furious and, as described in the book, his eyes were rolling in blood. Hanuman answered the various questions posed to him and quite candidly delivered his message. He almost came through as condescending when he advised *Ravana* as to what would be the correct and honourable course of action for the king to take. The explanation and its tone incensed the court further. How dare Hanuman challenge the mighty Ravana in his own court? Was there no limit to his insolence? Courtiers started to bay for Hanuman to be executed for all the destruction he had wrought. Their demand of their king to kill Hanuman reached a deafening crescendo.

All that the king had to do was to pronounce his decision and the task would be completed immediately. Nobody seemed opposed to the decision and, anyway, if at all anyone was opposed, how could he communicate his opposition in such a charged atmosphere?

Vibhishana was the younger brother of Ravana. He was deeply loyal to the king and always followed the path of righteousness. He was in disagreement with his elder brother's act of kidnapping Sita, and had openly advised his brother to desist from that path. So far he had not succeeded in persuading Ravana. Instead, he was in the bad books of the king.

With the impending decision to execute Hanuman, Vibhishana felt that a second unjust act was about to be done. According to *his* understanding of the royal diplomatic code of practices, a messenger can never be executed or killed, whatever be the provocation. A messenger can at the worst be punished, but not killed. And here was Ravana, about to break the well-established code of practices. But how could he express his disagreement in such a volatile atmosphere?

Vibhishana mustered courage and said, 'May the king be pleased to forgive. Please abandon anger and listen to what I have to say. No great king would inflict capital punishment on a messenger. You are acquainted with all that is virtuous and know all that constitutes right conduct. Please abandon your anger and reconsider what is right and what is wrong. It behoves a great king like you to do only what is appropriate.'

Ravana was incensed by what Vibhishana said, but he also saw the merit in his brother's supplication. For the moment he relented. He ordered that Hanuman be punished by setting alight his tail.

Later on, Ravana expelled Vibhishana from his kingdom. Being a strong believer in the path of righteousness, Vibhishana went to Rama and sought shelter, which he immediately got. Being a member of Rama's entourage made him a valuable ally to pass on information on the secrets of Ravana's army, its organisation and its vulnerabilities. For this reason some contemporary commentators opined that Vibhishana betrayed his brother.

Vibhishana was in disagreement on a matter of principle and ethics. His disagreement was not a difference of opinion or judgment on a particular factual matter. Neither was it based on ego and relationships. He felt he could not be silent when the disagreement was on a matter of principle. He spoke up with as much diplomacy as he could. He praised before he disagreed. He had to state his disagreement with clarity and he did so, but in the process he lost his position in the court and got expelled from the kingdom.

Vibhishana's method of disagreeing had the desired effect: Hanuman was spared and not killed. Otherwise the course of the Ramayana would have been very different. But *Vibhishana* could not avoid the king banishing him, perhaps not only for this disagreement but for also discouraging the king in his blind pursuit of Sita.

Archer Blood and Richard Nixon—a matter of principle

Pakistan had been carved out of an undivided India in 1947. It comprised two parts separated by more than a thousand miles. The eastern part of Pakistan was called East Bengal, later to become independent as Bangladesh.

The history of American geopolitics and policies in South Asia is complex and long. During the 1950s, Dwight Eisenhower was president of the United States and Richard Nixon his vice president. Nixon had visited India and Pakistan on a trip in 1953 and he did not take a liking to Nehru. According to him, Nehru railed 'obsessively and interminably' about Pakistan. Nixon thought of Nehru as being 'arrogant, abrasive, and suffocatingly self-righteous.'

After the India visit concluded, Nixon went to Pakistan. He found the people there to be staunchly anti-communist and pro-American. 'Pakistani people have fewer complexes than the Indians,' he observed. He expressed the view that Pakistan is a country he would like to do everything for.

Archer Kent Blood was born in Chicago in 1923. After his studies, he joined the United States Foreign Service in 1947. For the next thirteen years he served in several countries, among them Greece, Algeria, Germany and Afghanistan. In 1960, Blood was selected for a posting in Dhaka as a junior political officer. He later recalled that much of his work related to relaying to his political masters the grievances of the Bengalis, who felt undermined and abused by West Pakistan. He felt that his observations on this subject to Washington annoyed his bosses, as they liked to believe 'that Pakistan was a stable, united country'.

Blood was a voracious reader. His wife remarked about

him after his death: 'He was an exact person. He could become interested in anything, but he wanted to know the exact facts.'

In 1970, Nixon had become president of the United States and Henry Kissinger his secretary of state. Indira Gandhi, Nehru's daughter, had become the prime minister of India by then and General Yahya Khan was the president of Pakistan. The relationships between these key players in this narrative are important to note.

Nixon did not vibe well with Indira Gandhi, who also did not seem to care much for him. On the other hand, Nixon spoke of General Khan with an uncharacteristic blend of admiration and affection. Meanwhile, Kissinger's singular grip on White House power was the stuff of legend among the diplomatic corps. The Indian ambassador once cattily pointed out, 'Kissinger, on his part, never misses an opportunity to emphasise and underscore his own importance.'

Blood's first tenure helped him a lot because a decade later he was posted back to Dhaka, this time as the consul general. In 1970, when Blood arrived in Dhaka for his second stint, the events behind the creation of Bangladesh were unfolding in the east. By sheer coincidence, the consul general's Dhaka team had people with unusual and gory names, and quite relevant to the unfolding events. Blood's deputy political officer was Andrew Killgore and his junior political officer was called Scott Butcher!

Nature struck a huge blow when, in November 1970, Cyclone Bhola hit Bangladesh. It was widely regarded as one of the deadliest tropical cyclones in recorded history. Half a million people were estimated to have died. Despite this devastation, elections were held in December 1970, for the first time in Pakistan since independence.

In 1970, Yahya Khan was the president of undivided Pakistan. At the head of a military government, he had decided to conduct general elections throughout the country and these elections were conducted some weeks after the cyclone. He was absolutely confident of the outcome. The general was shocked by the outcome.

It is pertinent to note that since its independence Pakistan had never had democratic elections. Tensions had grown between the Punjabi-dominated western part of the country and the Bengali-dominated eastern part ever since independence, especially on the subject of whether the east was getting its due share of economic benefits. The Awami League, a regional party, progressively got strong in East Pakistan under its charismatic leader, Sheikh Mujibur Rehman.

The Awami League won the 1970 elections in the eastern region by a compelling and overwhelming majority. East Pakistan started asking for a lot more autonomy within the nation state. Those in West Pakistan did not like the ambitions of the eastern region. They suppressed their eastern citizens in many ways and did not give effect to the election results. The situation exploded.

Terrible atrocities were perpetrated by the Pakistan army on the Bengalis. It used American-supplied firearms and war equipment to conduct genocide on its own countrymen. General A.A.K. Niazi, the commander of the Pakistan forces in the east, wrote in his later years about the operations there in chilling words: 'The killing of civilians and scorched-earth policies...a display of stark cruelty, more merciless than the massacres...by Changez Khan or by the British at Jallianwala Bagh.' According to a Pakistani brigadier, one West Pakistan general asked his soldiers, 'How many Bengalis have we shot?'

Archer Blood witnessed the genocide of the Bengalis first-hand. He wrote incessantly to the powers in Washington, once, for example: 'The whole objective of the West Pakistan army apparently was and is to hit hard and terrorise the population into submission.' Blood was telling his bosses what they just did not want to hear. For sure, the White House disliked Blood's messages.

Two weeks into the slaughter, Blood and several officers of the consulate office sent a telegram to the White house in which they strongly and unequivocally expressed their dissent with American foreign policy. 'Numerous officers here consider it their duty to register strong dissent with the fundamental aspects of this policy,' the telegram stated. 'Our government has evidenced what many will consider moral bankruptcy…salvage our nation's position as a moral leader of the free world.'

Nixon and Kissinger felt very bitter. They reckoned that the Blood telegram was an act of unbearable insolence. On some other occasion, Nixon had written, 'We never fire anybody. We always promote the sons of bitches that kick us in the ass…when a bureaucrat deliberately thumbs his nose, we are going to get him.' The president complained about Blood and his brood to his cabinet, 'We have a lot of little people who love to be heroes.'

Nixon ordered the transfer of Blood from Dhaka. Blood morosely departed Dhaka by mid-1971. When Blood's superior at the state department asked him what he would like to do next, Blood replied crisply that, of course, he would like to run an embassy. Blood recalled later than even a proposal to run the irrelevant embassy in Upper Volta was shot down!

'For the next six years, while Kissinger was still in power, I was in professional exile, excluded from any work having to do with foreign policy,' recalled Blood. He plodded along for another ten years and finally, in 1982, in a despondent state, he retired from the American Foreign Service. In 2004, at the age of eighty-one, Blood passed away. The American embassy in Dhaka named its library for him.

It does appear that Archer Blood was a man of ethics and principles. He weighed up the implications of his speaking up and he seemed to know the consequences. He had seen what he had seen and seemed to know what he had to do. There was no way that he could have known what was being spoken about him in Washington. Later on, it was revealed that Kissinger referred to him as 'that maniac from Dhaka'.

His colleagues opined that there was nothing at all maniacal about Blood. He was a good product of the state department, a loyal officer and a conservative human being. One of them described Blood as 'a man of honour. For him there was a worse thing than losing his career. Had he not done what he did, he would have lost his honour'.

Archer Blood risked everything to express his disagreement with United States policy in East Bengal purely on a matter of principle and human ethics.

R.K. Talwar and Sanjay Gandhi—an ethical principle

Sanjay Gandhi was the second son of Indira Gandhi and the grandson of Jawaharlal Nehru. Being a scion of India's first family, he had a privileged upbringing. Sanjay was not known to be a diligent student in his school days. As he grew up he developed a fascination for cars. Perhaps he had inherited that from his father, Feroze Gandhi, who had a small Morris that he kept spotlessly black. Feroze would often polish the car and uncover its bonnet. Sanjay would work with his father on the car and the father would explain a few things to the young lad.

As Sanjay grew into adulthood, he showed an inclination to make cars for India. To improve his understanding of cars, an apprenticeship was arranged for him to train at the Rolls-Royce factory in Crewe, England. Sanjay's stint in Crewe was unremarkable except that once he was arrested for driving without a valid driving license, and on another occasion he somersaulted his car on the motorway. His general image was one of impatience and brashness.

One of his fellow apprentices later recalled Sanjay as 'an interesting person to know...I didn't like him because of his inflexibility...he argued with other apprentices a lot.' Sanjay left the apprenticeship with one year remaining of the course because, as he told a friend, 'I have learned everything there is to learn. I would be wasting my time if I were to stay any longer.'

When Sanjay returned to India, a public policy debate on the manufacture of a small car was raging. Sanjay expressed his desire to make a small car for India and his intent was officially announced in 1968 by the Ministry of Industrial Development. Within a few years the nationalised banks were arm-twisted by Indira Gandhi and her finance ministry to keep lending money to Sanjay's venture. The lending went on to such ridiculous levels that the Reserve Bank of India's deputy governor had to instruct the chairmen of nationalised banks 'not to advance further money to' Sanjay's venture. The Central Bank of India's chairman, Taneja, followed the instruction and was fired from his job for the effort.

In 1975, Indira Gandhi's government declared a national emergency in India. Democracy, elections, the free press, civic rights and so on took a back seat and a state of near terror followed for several months. This condition allowed non-constitutional authorities like Sanjay to flourish temporarily and he became a power centre. Sanjay had a long memory of those who were helpful to him and those who were not.

An episode occurred during the emergency with respect to a cement company, and was described in great detail in a speech by a contemporary (N. Vaghul). The cement company had borrowed money from the State Bank of India and had become sick. Seeing mismanagement as the problem, the bank agreed to restructure the loan, provided that it would change the promoter chief executive. Since the promoter knew Sanjay Gandhi, he sought his intervention. Sanjay rang the finance minister and asked him to ensure that the condition of changing the chief executive would be waived by the bank.

The finance minister spoke to the bank chairman, R.K. Talwar, who updated himself with the facts of the case and satisfied himself that he could not change the decision. He duly informed the minister. Upon being told this, Sanjay summoned Talwar, who refused to meet him as he had no authority to summon him. Sanjay gave instructions that Talwar be sacked, but there was a technical hitch: under the SBI Act, the chairman could not be sacked without sufficient cause. The finance minister, in an attempt to salvage a hopeless situation, offered Talwar a different assignment, as chairman of the banking commission. This was declined by Talwar, who offered to do both jobs if the minister so desired. The minister admitted that he faced a dilemma due to the inflexibility of Talwar and 'pressure from the highest quarters'.

Sanjay next set the Central Bureau of Investigation (CBI) to cook up corruption charges against Talwar. The CBI could not accomplish this. Finally, Sanjay asked that the SBI Act be amended in order to facilitate the sacking of Talwar. This came to be known as the 'Talwar amendment'.

With Parliament unable to play its natural and vigorous role, the bill was rubber-stamped and the stage was set for Talwar's sacking. He was once more given the choice to resign, but Talwar was defiant. He was given thirteen months' notice pay and compulsorily retired.

As his acolyte, N. Vaghul, later wrote in a booklet: 'Talwar departed from the bank at his usual time of 5.30 pm. There was nobody to see him off. In fact, everybody was scared to be associated with him...I walked across to meet him at his home.' Talwar told Vaghul, 'Look at the divine will. What a pleasure it is to be gifted with such divine blessings...as far as I am concerned, I am only an instrument of the divine and his will... The work in the bank is over. What the divine has in store for me I do not know.'

Talwar was an ardent devotee of The Mother at Auroville, which is where he retired to after his long banking career. Talwar narrated to his friend, V.A. George, how he felt about the Sanjay

Gandhi episode:

'Throughout my service of 33 years, I had been, from the outset, a fighter against arbitrariness. I had, over the years, established working practices to ensure that no arbitrary decisions were taken in any matter in the bank, particularly where the interests of an employee was involved. I had never known the true value that could be put on the maintenance of this practice over the years. The incident that I had gone through was surely an example of extreme arbitrariness.

'Thanks to the Mother, I remained calm throughout this ordeal. I had no grudge against anybody, not even the government or the prime minister. I believed that I was carrying out the will of the Mother and that the Mother had, through this incident, shown me the value of the battle I had waged against arbitrariness all these years.'

Talwar passed away at the age of ninety in Pondicherry. Glowing tributes were paid to him at his passing.

Disagree without becoming disagreeable

There is an art involved in how to disagree and express differences without becoming disagreeable. No institution trains one to discharge this role. It is among the most delicate among leadership challenges. What all such cases show is that if you stand up for something on a genuine principle, you may win the battle but you could lose the war. That does not mean that leaders must not stand up. One person's act of courage may well appear an act of foolishness to another.

These stories illustrate the true nature of courage—that you just have to do what you feel you need to do, irrespective of whether you personally win or lose. And how you view the same facts depend on which set of lenses sits on your nose pad!

9

Trust: The Fourth Lens

'To love is to suffer. To avoid suffering one must not love. But then one suffers from not loving. Therefore, to love is to suffer; not to love is to suffer; to suffer is to suffer.'

—Woody Allen, actor, director and writer

In the chapter on authenticity, there was a narration of the differences of opinion between Subhas Chandra Bose and Mahatma Gandhi. Their relationship, it would appear, progressively deteriorated. For the two of them, the divergence in political views must have resulted in a mutual loss of trust, perhaps even the perception of the other person being not authentic. Howsoever, in general the mere fact of a difference of opinion does not imply a lack of trust.

Listening to others and trying to accommodate diverse views inevitably mean that differences will be experienced. Trust can coexist with differences. If the boss has consulted many employees, he or she cannot implement everybody's opinion. If he or she has taken a different course of action than the one suggested by a particular individual, that person is likely to feel ignored. Ignoring some views is inevitable when the boss has to choose from myriad viewpoints. Transformational leaders accommodate differences but do not let them interfere with personal relations or action.

How trust was built in tribal societies

Trust and distrust are essential components of social functioning. Society would be paralysed without trust.

Anthropologist Bronislaw Malinowsky has studied the Trobriand islanders of the Pacific in an investigation. He found that in an encounter of unknown people, trust is created by one side offering a gift (this may be why the Japanese practice of gifting exists). Since trust builds out of reciprocity, the other side also offers a gift. In this way gifts accumulate on both sides and these are passed on in a circular manner of gifting. It reminds one of the practice at birthday parties where children bring a gift for the birthday child and take back a reciprocal gift.

Cast your mind back to many, many years ago when the world was inhabited by primitive societies. There is a comparative study of two kinds of ancient tribal people, the Shoshone in North America and the Kung San in the African Kalahari. Both lived in barren; one ate shrubs and roots and the other ate large animals. There is a contrast between their different social evolutions.

The Shoshone people used to inhabit the Great Basin of North America, corresponding roughly to present-day Nevada. Sociologists found that theirs was a very simple society, where the basic social organisation was the family and the male head represented the 'total legal and political' system. It was as though a Shoshone family could live all its life by itself with very little interaction or interdependence with other such family units.

Shoshone families would typically do it alone, roaming the desert with a bag and a digging stick, searching for roots and seeds. It seemed that their ambitions were small and so too the resources they deployed to realise these ambitions. They matched one with the other and lived extremely simple lives, with equally simple social structures. There was no big game to hunt for but occasionally they would spot some delicious jackrabbits.

This reflected a higher level of ambition. To enjoy this delicacy they would employ a net hundreds of feet long; in this the rabbits were herded before being clubbed to death. A single family could not handle this net, so on an opportunistic basis a dozen or so Shoshone families would come together and cooperate under a rabbit boss. After enjoying the spoils of their cooperation together, they would revert to the more traditional structure of the family unit.

In contrast the Kung San, also a desert people, evolved very differently. The Kung San ate giraffe meat. A simple, small family unit could not possibly overcome a large giraffe, so a complex form of social cooperation evolved. Ways were found to assemble larger groups. Indeed, there might have been a surplus beyond the need to satisfy immediate hunger.

Having no preservation techniques, the Kung San may have invited 'non-contributing' members to join the feast, creating an obligation to be discharged on some other occasion. This would further contribute to a more complex social structure. When the resources fell short of what was required to realise the ambition, people cooperated to do something about it. Cooperation was thus fostered by a higher ambition.

What generates trust?

Among the many stories that permeate the Tata environment, one pertains to an incident involving group chairman JRD Tata and senior Tata director A.D. Shroff in the early 1950s. The incident involved a heated exchange between JRD and Shroff during a board meeting of Tata Sons. It appears that JRD referred to a view expressed by Shroff as 'a dishonest opinion'. Shroff felt offended that he had been referred to as being dishonest. The incident threatened the continuation of Shroff's association with Tata. Shroff sent in his resignation but the matter was patched up by JRD with a great sense of egalitarianism and humility.

This is what JRD wrote in a letter to Shroff dated August 23, 1951:

'I was surprised and upset at receiving your letter. I do not remember exactly the words I used during the somewhat heated exchange at the agents' meeting, but my complaint to you was merely that an argument you used to score a debating point over me was not an honest one. That is surely a far cry from questioning your honesty and I am surprised that you interpreted it in that way.

'You have a right to resent my speaking angrily or showing you discourtesy as a result, and for that I sincerely apologize, but if friends and associates decided to part every time they had an argument, life would become very difficult.

'You refer to my firm. Except that I am personally a relatively minor shareholder, I don't think there is any difference on that account in any of us. We all work for it and we should think of it as our firm. The trouble with both of us is that we both have a hell of a temper!'

Shroff did not press his resignation. In fact he served Tata thereafter in his old spirit of trust.

Authenticity is the currency one uses to generate trust. An individual tries to 'know' another person; as he or she gets to know more, the individual assesses whether there is any zone of common interest. Put another way, the two individuals trade their 'authenticity chips'. If there is no commonality then a casual sort of relationship develops. If there emerges a deep common interest, say through work or sports, a specialised relationship blooms in that field, trustworthy or otherwise. People say 'He is my golf friend' or 'She is my bridge friend'. If the two people have several touch points over a wide range of subjects, a more total relationship develops. It may be with lots of trust, a little trust or actual distrust.

All relationships are subject to what the sociologist Bo Rothstein has called social traps. Every society has certain givens as perceptions, and some are near universal; for example, the view that politicians are untrustworthy, that public officials are corrupt, or that business folks are dishonest. These perceptions are called the social traps, which influence whether we trust someone, and the way that we trust.

The presence of trust in a relationship is a great energiser, just as much as its absence creates loss of morale. Human unhappiness emanates from the absence of trust. The roots of conflict between work and family also lie in the soil called trust. For instance, in a work situation a person may be in the inner-most circle of trust with the boss at a point of time. After some time one may find oneself in a middle circle or even in an outer circle. These are well illustrated in the trajectories traversed by Bose with Gandhi. Such variations in trust cause executives great tension and grief.

The opposite of such behaviour is also possible. An example from history is of how a seemingly close, trusting relationship was destroyed by an emergent distrust in the new Russian state during the early Bolshevik days.

How trust is destroyed: Bolshevik Russia

I used to visit the erstwhile Soviet Union, Poland, Romania and other communist states frequently for business during the 1980s. I would wonder how the system managed to create such a spooky state. I would be warned by well-wishers not to say anything and to behave with utmost care in hotel lobbies and in public places. I never found out if those warnings were well-founded. Out of abundant caution, I followed them, thus fostering a social trap. Finding out more about secretiveness in Moscow was hardly possible.

Many years later, I found an account of the circumstances, which partially explained the spooky state. Geoffrey Hosking is emeritus professor of Russian history at University College, London. In his book, *Trust: A History* (New York, 2014), he analyses the situation in the Soviet Union.

In the 1930s, Soviet leaders were plagued by acute dilemmas of trust and distrust. The Bolsheviks had successfully ousted the Tsar through their revolution in 1917. Soon after the Tsar was displaced, there followed a civil war. The situation produced stressful circumstances for the revolutionaries.

During Tsarist times, society was dominated by rich people who were indifferent to the suffering of the Russian poor. During the revolution against the decrepit Tsarist system, whatever the differences may have been among the revolutionaries, they were united by a strong sense of mutual dependence and trust. This trust was constantly challenged by the pressures of the struggle. After the Bolsheviks revolted successfully, the inner contradictions of the erstwhile colleagues started showing up, resulting in apprehensions about groups and factionalism. (Does all this not happen within companies when colleagues grow together for decades and become good social friends, yet they fall apart when they start to compete for the few and key senior jobs?)

Joseph Stalin, the ruthless Soviet leader, dealt with the situation in the harshest possible manner. Sergei Kirov, the first secretary of the Leningrad Party, was mysteriously assassinated. Leon Trotsky was not only expelled from the party but also from the country. Nikolai Bukharin and Stalin had been colleagues before and during the Bolshevik revolution of 1917 and both had belonged to the party's central committee. But Stalin jailed Bukharin, who wrote a letter to Stalin in December 1937. He was, of course, seeking a pardon and he addressed Stalin like a close friend, not as the supreme ruler of Soviet Russia which Stalin had become.

Mikhail Prishvin, a supportive Soviet writer, wrote in October 1937, 'People have completely stopped trusting each other. They devote themselves to work and do not even whisper to each other.'

This narrative is not to recount Russian history, but to demonstrate how trust can break down rapidly in a society or an institution. Trust and distrust are at the foundational level of any society, company or institution. It is not possible to lead a coherent life without trust; distrust can lead to a very difficult life.

How distrust develops

Politicians, business leaders and other public personalities often are dependent on the trust of their constituencies in order to remain effective. Such people have a particularly delicate balance to accomplish. There are many stories of leaders who have lost trust, testament to the adage that it is so difficult to earn trust and so utterly easy to lose it. I choose a century-old story, that of Charles Stewart Parnell, to illustrate.

Parnell led the Irish Parliamentary Party for sixteen years, from 1875 and 1891. Through his family he possessed an extraordinary number of prestigious links to members of Irish society; he had a privileged upbringing. But it was as the leader of Irish nationalism that Parnell established his fame. He was credited with many significant political contributions, and the Irish people loved and respected him. Parnell was a perfect leader as people viewed him through their six lenses of the work eye.

Viewed through the second eye of relationships, he faltered at one stage of his career when, coincidentally, he was pretty much at his peak. Parnell took up residence with a lady, one who was planning to separate from her husband. Parnell was a Protestant in a constituency full of Roman Catholics. For them divorce was unacceptable. Parnell fell from grace. The incident must be viewed by the standards of the day in that society. Parnell soon lost the support for his leadership. Despite all that, Parnell is held out as 'one of the greatest men of the nineteenth century' and as 'the strongest man that the House of Commons has seen in a century-and-a-half.'

Such incidents occur routinely nowadays and the consequences can be similar. Although social mores have changed dramatically, in many apparently modern and liberal societies infidelity and divorce are perceived negatively. Political and business confidence tends to be fragile if leaders are touched by such perceived imperfections. An interesting and sober aspect of trust is that followers expect their leaders to be paragons of virtue, even while knowing that such people are a fiction of their imagination.

Using William Ury's model on conflict resolution, as described by him in *The Third Side: Why We Fight and How We Can Stop* (New York, 2000), the stages of a developing distrust can be mapped. First there are latent tensions, which are issue-based; these are the kind of differences that arise from different viewpoints and daily pressures. In the second stage the conflicts become more overt. If the overt conflicts are handled well, they stay within boundaries, but if the conflicts are mishandled personal resentment starts to replace issue-based differences. This may lead to the third stage, when people give up on each other and some start to withdraw from the relationship. As withdrawal occurs, assumptions and stereotypes start to abound. Finally the situation transforms into a gridlock, when hostile parties may even risk their own survival rather than let the other side win.

Winning trust is easy, nurturing trust is hard work, and keeping trust is very difficult. It is far easier to lose trust than to work hard to maintain trust. You have to use three vectors or levers to nurture trust.

Three trust vectors: feeling, attitude and relationships

As Professor Hosking points out, it is difficult to study trust because it 'is several phenomena at once'.

Trust has three vectors or attributes. It is, first of all, a *feeling*: a person feels no insecurity to speak or act. Secondly, it is an *attitude*: an expectation about a person or institution that is taken for granted; for example, you expect that the pilot will land the plane safely, or that water will emerge from the tap when you turn it on. Third and last, it is a *relationship* between two people or groups of people; for example, a family or community will hang together or that a marriage will imply fidelity.

Organisations like Gallup generate statistics through their polls to show that trust within society and institutions is declining, and in some instances has reached perilously low levels. By way of illustration, there is universally a great distrust of politicians. Distrust among colleagues in a company results in employees getting emotionally disengaged with their employer. When the aggregate attitude shifts from scepticism to suspicion, the conditions for a breakdown start to assemble.

In the 1990s, a Russian tax inspector was amazed at the tax compliance of Swedes. How on earth this could happen, considering that Russia was exactly the opposite. The answer was that most Swedes paid their taxes because they believed that every Swede did, and also that the tax collections would be honestly spent. The Russian observed that the exact opposite was true in Russia. Every Russian suspected that other Russians did not pay tax and, anyway, the collected tax was not spent honestly.

'Social traps produce obstinately vicious circles of distrust from which escape is extremely difficult,' according to Hosking. Many emerging markets are standing examples of this phenomenon.

The opposite of a social trap can also occur. If a person evokes trust through his or her behaviour and also represents a trusted institution, the synergy can be multiplicative. The story that follows is of Geeta, who raises funds in an extraordinarily committed way for the Tata Medical Centre in Kolkata. In the context of this social trap, raising funds for a genuine social cause on a continuous basis requires all the three vectors earlier referred to—feeling, attitude and relationships—and that as an act of love rather than for remuneration.

Building trust in an atmosphere of distrust

In India the maximum incidence of specific cancers occurs in the eastern part of the country. Many of those so affected happen to be children. It is a tragic situation. The need for an effective treatment centre in the east was a crying one in society for a long, long time. Tata set up a Tata Medical Centre in Kolkata in 2008 at a cost of about Rs 350 crore, fully paid for by the Tata Trusts and various Tata companies.

The Tata Medical Centre, an ultra-modern hospital with a hugely talented group of doctors and staff. One of the mandates of the hospital is to reserve close to half of its beds for free treatment for the underprivileged. This means that the hospital has to raise public donations as a corpus or on an annualised and ongoing contribution to defray the expenses of the free treatment.

Fund raising for charity in India is generally hampered by the social trap that people do not believe that the funds are deployed honestly. Money is either illegitimately siphoned off or too much of the money is spent in administering the fund rather than deploying it for the target purpose. In Indian politics there is a famous quotation, attributed to former Prime Minister Rajiv Gandhi, that barely 20 per cent of the money for social missions reaches the target.

In an earlier chapter, Nihal Kaviratne's story was recounted. The success of St Jude in raising funds illustrated that there is great generosity in India for honest-spending charities. I reckon that the situation exists in many societies: generosity is directly proportional to the belief and trust that the donations will be deployed honestly.

An additional challenge in raising the funds for the Kolkata hospital was that potential donors wanted to know why Tata would not pay for the free treatment as well, apart from having paid the capital cost and the running costs of the hospital. In one sense the expectation was a tribute to the generosity of the House of Tata, which has a fabulous track record, built up over a century, of spending generously for the community and society. In another sense it was the general reluctance of donors to pay for causes where they were unsure of how honestly their donation would be spent.

The hospital engaged professional fund-raising consultants for a couple of years, but the results were not fruitful. It had to consider alternative ways to tap into the generosity of institutions and public. On a particular evening, one of the trustees witnessed a small but imaginative fund-raising show at the Sophia School for Special Children. He enquired about the people behind the show and learnt that the creative person was an advertising professional called Geeta. The trustee was impressed and became instrumental in appointing Geeta to get involved with the hospital's mission. Geeta refused to accept remuneration and insisted on working for a token reward of Rs 101 per year.

The communications programme was centred on appealing to people's hearts, not to their minds. Trust is more a heart matter than a mind matter. The programme got off to a great start and delivered significant results. The hospital leadership felt positive after Geeta joined the hospital as honorary director (donor relations) in 2011. From scratch she built a team of few to assist her and the hospital director in the task. In around five years she and her team raised Rs 140 crore for the hospital. Without doubt her efforts were considerably aided by the enormous reputation of Tata as an honest institution.

Geeta's story and mission become relevant in this chapter on trust. In a society where charity money is widely believed to be misused, how did she build trust, what made her do it, what was the reward for her? (Disclosure: Geeta is my wife, but I would hope that that is no reason to eliminate her story.)

Geeta's trust vectors: feeling, attitude and relationships

Apart from her parents, Geeta's grandparents were huge influences in shaping her in the growing-up years in Hyderabad. She is an only child. Because her father was in a transferable job, she spent several of her growing-up years with her grandparents in Hyderabad. She recalls three strong influences of the grandparents from both sides of her family.

First, generosity to an extreme, almost extravagant level. Both her grandfathers became successful lawyers in Hyderabad, and both had come up from exceptionally humble beginnings. Their sudden entry into economic prosperity and social status never allowed them to forget their humble origins. Indigent and less fortunate relatives would visit their home to seek help and favours. From the early 1930s right into Geeta's childhood years, the family kitchen was operational all the time. Near and distant relatives would arrive, often without notice.

Sometimes food would be cooked at home and sent in containers to hospitals to feed the poor. As a child Geeta was amazed at the uncertainty and chaos all this created in the household routine. It seemed to rob the family of its private time. Geeta's grandmothers taught her the lesson that to give generously for the care of less privileged relations and people is a responsibility.

Second, faith in God and spirituality. The grandparents

supported both home and community prayers on a regular and wide scale. They donated generously to far-flung temples. One grandmother was referred to by temple priests as 'Sri Dharma Chudamani', which literally means 'the jewel of righteousness'. Although a little girl, Geeta was encouraged by her grandparents to learn several of the scriptures in Tamil and Sanskrit at home. Despite the social discouragement to girls reciting Vedic chants, the child Geeta would join experienced priests as they recited the Vedas at religious functions.

Third is a terrible memory of the loss of a dear uncle to cancer. He suffered from Hodgkin's disease and there was no cure. As a young girl in their joint family home, she would try to cheer him up. But he was always cheerful on his own because he had learned to accept the inevitable. The episode caused grief on a massive scale to child Geeta and she was shaken to tears. Finally the end came. At a young age Geeta had to learn to fight back tears and despair.

It is noteworthy that Geeta recalls generosity, spirituality and sorrow (from cancer) as the dominant influences of her childhood. What about birthday parties, movies and the like? 'Good girls do not go to birthday parties, so do not grumble. God is everything and you must learn to surrender to Him,' her grandmothers would say. Geeta's family was, clearly, extremely conservative and orthodox.

Not surprisingly Geeta got married in a traditional arranged marriage when she was twenty. From her orthodox upbringing she found herself pitched into a far more modern family environment.

She recalls: 'My father-in-law worked in the corporate sector, unlike anyone in my family; while he was comfortable in a *veshti* at home, at official functions he sported a bow tie, held a cigarette in one hand and a glass of Scotch whisky in the other. My mother-in-law encouraged me to go out and work, supported by an approving nod from my husband. One sister-in-law had a pilot's licence, another was a regular columnist in the newspapers. Gosh, I lacked self-confidence to do anything! However, I was encouraged by my in-laws into going out to work rather than sit at home. They did this by almost shaming me.'

Geeta could write and she could talk effortlessly. She had a way with words. She decided instinctively to exploit this strength by teaching in a school. Geeta was modestly successful. Teaching gave her some self-esteem but she yearned for something that was more creative, that would bring her more satisfaction. She enrolled for a course on marketing and advertising. It gave her access to advertising agencies.

Geeta had a younger cousin who was mentally challenged. She had observed how her aunt and uncle bore their responsibility with peace and calm, doing what they had to for their child without ever thinking about it as a burden. Geeta was moved by their spirituality and their sense of duty without reward—the karmic principle, as the Bhagavad Gita preaches. She was attracted to and got associated with a school for the mentally challenged (Sadhana School, Mumbai) and its charismatic principal, Sister Gaitonde.

After a few short work stints at some advertising agencies, Geeta did a copy test at Trikaya Grey Advertising, headed then by Ravi Gupta. In a sort of final interview, Ravi asked her what she really wanted to do in her life. How did she see herself two years, five years and ten years later in her professional life?

Geeta's response was spontaneous, 'In two years I would like to be an employee of your agency, but doing more for Sadhana School,' she said. 'Nobody thinks of the underprivileged; we are all busy making more money, isn't it?' The humanist that he was, Ravi responded with alacrity: not only would Geeta have the job, but Trikaya Grey would place all its resources at advancing her vision without any charge to the cause. For Geeta this was an epiphany. She could enjoy doing what she wanted and, on top of that, she would be paid for it!

It was a turning point in Geeta's life. She would experience what it is 'to enjoy what she would do and do what she enjoyed', true nirvana. Geeta had found her metier, her purpose in life; now there would be no looking back. And, God be praised, that is the way it panned out.

Geeta spent seventeen long and absolutely joyful years at Trikaya. She wrote radio jingles, press copy headlines, film scripts and did all sorts of creative stuff, while finding the energy and time to work with Sister Gaitonde and the Sadhana School. During this period she had two more stressful experiences with cancer. Her dear colleague Sunita Vaswani contracted cancer at the young age of thirty. Sunita withered away under Geeta's agonised gaze. For Geeta this was her second brush with cancer, her dear uncle being the first. She was shattered.

And then came yet another blow from cancer: her dear friend, Amina Halim of Kolkata, who fought cancer bravely for an extended period, finally succumbed. On a grey and sombre afternoon at Kolkata, Amina seemed to say her farewells and set out for her final destination, leaving Geeta devastated. 'Oh, what is this cancer that has taken away an uncle, a dear work colleague and a wonderful friend from me? Is there only darkness around? Is there any way to shed light for those affected?' Geeta wept uncontrollably. But what had to happen, happened. Three deaths of people close to her from cancer, seemingly a disease without reprieve.

Worse was to come for Geeta. In the late 1990s, her father, a non-smoker, succumbed to lung cancer. Four near and dear ones had fallen to cancer during a fifteen-year period.

During her soul-searching years, Geeta ran into a redoubtable lady called Sarla Kohli in Bangalore. Kohli worked relentlessly to alleviate cancer through her local leadership of the Cancer Patients' Association. Kohli asked Geeta to join her in fundraising;

she asked her to step out of the small-time targets she worked towards and think bigger. With her inspiration, Geeta staged fundraising shows at Bangalore—including one with actor and director Farhan Akhtar—through which she raised Rs 1.5 crore for the cause.

Geeta was on a roll now, as she says, with the initial prodding of Sister Gaitonde and, later, with the massive inspiration of Kohli. She learnt to think more ambitiously, not for herself but for the causes she worked on. On one occasion, Sister Gaitonde gave her an invaluable piece of advice: wealthy people may have large hearts but common people have the largest hearts.

At a Sadhana School fundraiser that Geeta helped organise, a trustee of the Tata Medical Centre was present. He was touched to the core by the endeavour. The trustee piloted a proposal through the Tata trusts to donate a substantial sum to the Sadhana School (to make up the corpus required for the school's expansion). Bravo to Tata, not just for the generosity, but, in the process and quite accidentally, giving wings to a new talent which they could devote time for the Tata Medical Centre.

Geeta had years ago quit advertising to devote all her time to the Sadhana School to help them achieve their expansion goals. Sister Gaitonde blessed her and advised her to follow the inspiration of God—to serve the Tata Medical Centre in Kolkata, not for a salary but for love.

Connecting the dots: childhood, emotions and empathy

It almost appears that fate or luck or some unseen Hand connected together some dots that brought Geeta to fund-raising for cancer. Among many, some of the dots were her emotions and feelings as one death after another occurred due to cancer, her childhood and upbringing to be giving rather than only taking, her capacity to feel inspired through positive psychology and her candour in facing up to her own vulnerabilities.

She lost her favourite uncle, Ramraju, to Hodgkins when she was all of eleven. As she remembers Ramraju, he was always cheerful, he could sing like a dream, he spoke like an orator. To her young mind, he was the near-perfect man. That he was a pleasant and personable individual must have had its own significance for a young child. Ramraju was literally being chewed up by a galloping cancer.

Geeta's grandparents never demonstrated their true feelings; they appeared to be perpetually stoic and prayerful, never once letting down their guard or demonstrating any concern. Geeta could not understand how they did so. She was like putty in the sense that as a child, she would feel depressed at the deteriorating condition of her uncle, but the adult in her was called upon to radiate positive energy rather than transmit negative feelings of depression. In fact, Geeta was sent away from her grandparents' home to school in another city, partly to save her young psyche the duality of living with completely opposite emotions with respect to her uncle. When Ramraju finally died, she was not around to say farewell; she was merely told the news later.

Years later she befriended her advertising colleague, Sunita Vaswani. It seems a surprise that Geeta could befriend a person like Sunita because no two people could be more poles apart. Geeta was the shy and conservatively brought-up young woman, learning to live the conventional, married life in Mumbai. Sunita was irreverent and completely the opposite. Sunita held her drink, smoked what she wanted to and came through as bohemian; as the Bombay expression goes, Sunita was completely *bindaas*.

Sunita would wear western clothes, jeans and sweat shirts, whereas Geeta would be dressed in more conventional Indian clothes and the characteristic Tamil *mallippu* flowers in her hair. Geeta would experiment with jeans and short hair styles. Sunita would chide her to remain who she best was. '*Yennamma*, you are who you are, you look gorgeous in a saree or salwar kameez with your sweet-smelling *mallipu*, why on earth are you trying to be somebody else?

Yet, just as opposite polarities attract, the two were deeply friendly. The very last thing that Geeta could imagine was that Sunita would be in a hospital. With tears in her eyes, Geeta recalls Sunita's bloated face and their last contacts at the Tata Memorial Hospital, Mumbai. Then one day, Sunita was gone, all alone and forever.

Then the 'serial killer' arrived to take Amina Halim. Geeta got to know about Amina and of Amina through a mutual friend while Geeta lived with her family in Saudi Arabia. Amina was from a wealthy Muslim family of Kolkata, a lawyer by profession. She was deeply conscious about the right of a woman to be ambitious and the woman's right to enjoy life sensibly, no less than any man. She had a bubbling personality that radiated positive psychology. She would talk to Geeta about her inner conflicts while professionally defending a person in a criminal case, knowing very well that the person had committed the crime in question. What would win—the profession or her opinion?

On one occasion Geeta wondered aloud about what previous birth connection there might have been between the two of them. Amina dismissed the thought by saying, 'I am a Muslim and I do not believe in rebirth.' Yet she would engage in conversations about whether their mutual care for each other could be compared to the proverbial Mohammed and Mehrunissa!

Amina was not the type who would succumb to cancer. She was a ferocious fighter, like the proverbial warrior, throwing everything she had, fighting till the very last. But the end came after the fight, as all ends do come. She almost appeared to tamely succumb to the 'serial killer,' secure in her thought that she had given the fight the very best that she could and very accepting of the inevitable outcome.

The next victim was her doting father. He was as pure as human beings come, especially when it came to cancer-connected habits. Not one cigarette, not a drop of alcohol, no wasting lifestyle even for a few aberrant years, prayers every morning as well as the evening, gentle as the snow, you cannot do better. Where on earth could the cancer attck such a man's lungs? Could it be other people's smoking? But who cared, he was the next victim to the killer. Geeta could bear it because he lived to his eighties, but his hallucinations and pitiable departing conditions were too stressful. Just like her grandparents withstood the inevitable with regard to Ramraju, her mother looked after her father, diligently and patiently, even though she fully well knew that *Yama* was snatching him away, day after day, succeeding by a few centimetres each day.

The list is longer. She was deeply affected by the loss to cancer of her mother-in-law, then her first boss, Ravi Gupta, and then a dear friend, Nilima Rovshen. These were too many cancer dots for her to cope with, and these experiences drove her into what psychologists call 'learned helplessness.'

Suddenly an unconnected dot appeared in the form of Sarla Kohli. Could she help with fund-raising for cancer in Bangalore? The authentic and true nature of a person shows up when the person is most vulnerable. Geeta joined Sarla Kohli's efforts and embellished Kohliji's institution by her efforts. She stumbled on the ever-so-simple-looking formula: bring your positive psychology, persuasive writing skills and emotional empathy for cancer patients into a new *menage e trois* act.

What is fascinating is not the story of Geeta; the fascinating aspect is how the six lenses of work and family coalesced in this instance—purpose, authenticity, courage, trust, luck and fulfilment—and came into focus. It was not planned; it was the hand of God or whatever you wish to call it. Work and family were not in conflict. They were a seamless extension of each other.

What would make an apparently shy, small-town, conservative girl grow into a persuasive, people-centred fundraiser? Which is the real Geeta?

'Both are the authentic Geeta, but at different points of time,' she explains. 'I stumbled on to the fact that I could use my creativity and persuasiveness for a cause different from myself. My grandparents had taught me generosity and spirituality as the way to overcome life's challenges. Here was an opportunity that blended those lessons. I could work for others' betterment, I could just be my true self and derive joy out of reducing, howsoever little, the pain felt by others. Is this not happiness?'

Everybody in the world tries to get happiness, most by earning more money, a higher position and status. A few, like Nihal and Geeta, earn and do what they think is right for their families and relationships. Somewhere they realise that true happiness is work without reward, what the Bhagavad Gita calls *nishkamya karma*.

Not many among us are capable of giving up everything for a cause. Only a few are able to do that, and the world is richer for such people. That said, there are many, many people who know when and how to give of themselves. They choose the timing and the manner. Nihal and Geeta (and many others whose stories I have not narrated) are examples. In the process, they create trust, which is the lubricant that enables society to stay coherent.

Trust is like ceramic. If it is made and if it stays strong, it serves its master for long. Once broken, it does not mend.

10

Luck: The Fifth Lens

> 'You know what luck is? Luck is believing that you are lucky, that's all…To hold a front position in this race, you've got to believe that you are lucky.'
>
> —Marlon Brando as Stanley Kowalski, *A Streetcar Named Desire*

The word luck has many adjacent attributes. Luck may be good or bad. Belief in luck may be a superstition. Taking a bet (for example on the stock market) or making a prediction about the future may turn out to be lucky or unlucky. Coincidences may be mistaken for luck, for example, Mr A was scheduled to take this flight but he cancelled last minute and that flight crashed. Luck has many symbolisms and attributes. These terms and expressions are the subject of this chapter. At the end, the idea of earned luck and unearned luck are brought in so that the relevance of luck can be understood in a sane way.

Napoleon's statement that he would choose a lucky general has been quoted many times over. The fifth lens through which we view events and people is the lens of luck. We don't want to admit that we believe in it, but secretly we do believe in luck. If we have to admit belief in luck, we don't mind admitting belief in bad luck, especially when it is to ourselves. With respect to others, we seem to recognise clearly what constitutes their good luck.

Psychologists have identified four moods produced by luck. If we have bad luck, we feel self-pity. If we have good luck, we feel happy or elated. If another person gets good luck, we feel jealous. If another person gets bad luck, we feel a mean sense of joy, what the Germans call schadenfreude.

We are tied up in a spaghetti of beliefs and concepts surrounding luck—coincidences, superstitions, predictions. We accept the concept of coincidence because we experience coincidences all the time. Coincidences may or may not have a cause and effect relationship. An example of a random coincidence: when I was born in 1945, the population of the world was three billion. Today it is seven billion. Clearly this statistic has nothing to do with my activities, it is a random coincidence.

Another example: during a conversation with me, Dr Jamshed Irani, former managing director of Tata Steel, told me 'For several years after my return from the UK and after I joined the erstwhile TISCO, I got no promotion. My father was then alive and he might have been a bit disappointed in those years. Then my father died after which I got six promotions. If he had been alive, he would have been very happy.'

No cause and effect, but a random coincidence.

However when someone says, 'I became CEO in 1981 and over the next ten years, sales went up at 30 per cent per annum,' he or she is subtly or overtly suggesting a cause and effect relationship.

Apart from the idea of luck and coincidence, humans have deep interest in predicting the future. What would we not do to know the future? Although we would readily admit in our rational moments that it is irrational to be superstitious, the fact is that we are superstitious. We become so in spite of our rationality and superstition can be all encompassing in controlling us.

Luck as a belief

The reader may consider the inclusion of luck as a lens to be unusual. The fact is that we believe in it in one sense, and dismiss it in another sense. Accepting the existence of luck is perceived as a sign of weakness in our turbulent times. Luck can also become a crutch for non-performance. Therefore organisations discourage any talk of luck. When positive things happen in an organisation, leaders are quick to point out that it is the fruit of consciously adopted strategies and great foresight. When things go awry, the same leaders would readily cite external factors. This was most visible in India between 2003 till 2009 when the country recorded strong growth. The ruling government attributed the growth to its policies. But the poor performance in the period 2010 onwards was attributed to the international crises like Lehman Brothers collapse and general volatility!

Author and academic, John Kay, criticizes the view that success in a business must be derived from a single, shaping vision or a mission statement that is relentlessly executed. It is wrong to imagine design when there was only adaptation and improvisation. It is wrong to attribute every success to some deliberate plan.

The same holds true for an individual's life. We are too easily misled by biographies of great people who, after the fact, claim to have meticulously planned their ascent. The origins of success are much too subtle and complex. Life does not follow a course and we change in many ways as we grow.

The Black Scholes formula pretended to replace mere gambling with hard science and therefore, you would be led to believe that you no more needed luck. As soon as the belief was accepted, Long Term Capital Management went bust in 1998.

Good outcomes are dressed up as strategic strokes of genius; catastrophes are attributed to bad luck. We all feel that there is something called luck, but it is not fashionable to admit it.

Admitting the existence of luck demands the acknowledgement that some things are beyond our control, and the control-freak side of human nature is never going to accept such an uncomfortable state of affairs without a fight.

Faith in experts

We are considerably swayed by experts on a subject. Their opinion on their subject matters to us and we tend to rely on those opinions. As social animals, we are exquisitely sensitive to status and an expert has considerable status. People love stories; they are rooted in the story of our evolution. Get acknowledged as an expert; be articulate, enthusiastic and authoritative. You can be a winner.

We believe expert predictions because we are hard-wired to avoid uncertainty. Fundamentally we believe because we want to believe. For humans, inventing stories that make the world sensible and orderly is as natural as breathing. Admitting a mistake and moving on does not come easily to homo-sapiens. The ability of the mind to fool itself by unconscious fudging on the facts is far greater than most people realize.

Those who place their predictions in the public domain often rue their impetuous act. For the examples that appear below, I owe a lot to author Dan Gardner who has chronicled several examples in his book *Future Babble* (New York, 2011).

Frailty of predictions

In the early 1900s, several experts were convinced that the world had evolved to the point that there could be no more wars.

In 1902, the great American economist John Bates Clark imagined himself in 2002, looking back on 100 years. 'There is certainly enough in our present condition to make our gladness overflow...The spirit of laughter and song may abide with us through the years that are coming...Nations bound by such economic ties as of now would never disrupt the great industrial organisation and start fighting.'

Esteemed British historian G.P. Gooch wrote in 1911, 'We can now look forward with something like confidence to the time when war between civilised nations will be as antiquated as a duel.'

Manchester Guardian journalist H.N. Brailsford was quite clear when he wrote, 'It is as certain as anything in politics can be, that the frontiers of our modern national states are finally drawn. My own belief is that there will be no more wars among the six Great Powers.' The First World War came about in 1914.

In 1967, two brothers, William and Paul Paddock, published a book entitled *Famine, 1975! America's Decision: What Will Survive?* (Boston, 1967). One was an agronomist and the other was a Foreign Service officer. In the book *The Population Bomb* (New York, 1968) Paul Ehrlich, a Stanford biologist, declared that 'the battle to feed all of humanity is over. In the 1970s, the world will undergo famines. Hundreds of missions of people will starve to death in spite of any crash program embarked upon as of now.' Biologist James Bonner wrote in *Science* magazine, 'All serious students agree that famine among the peoples of the underdeveloped world is inevitable. The USDA sees 1985 as the beginning of the years of hunger.'

Luckily all these dire predictions came to nought. As IMF economist Prakash Loungani wrote, 'The economists' record of failure to predict recessions is virtually unblemished. Economists are the least accurate when they are most needed.'

Of Toynbee's great work of history *A Study of History*, historians were critical. A.J.P. Taylor said, 'The events of the past can be made to prove anything if they are arranged in a suitable pattern, and Professor Toynbee has succeeded in forcing them into a scheme that was in his head from the beginning.'

Mauritius won independence from Britain in 1968. Two Nobel Prize Winners were pessimistic about its ability to pull out of poverty. V.S. Naipaul said that the problems of Mauritius defy solutions. James Meade, a Cambridge economist, said 'it would be a great achievement' if Mauritius ever found employment for all its population. An American expert had predicted a future of 'famines, epidemics and martial law.'

Yet Mauritius evolved into a model of multi-cultural co-existence.

The fox and the hedgehog

Greek poet Archilocus wrote, 'The fox knows many things but the hedgehog knows one big thing.'

Philip Tetlock was a psychology professor at Haas Business School. His experiments showed that experts were as accurate as random guesses. Among experts he found that one group was somewhat more accurate than another group. The first group (foxes) was self-critical, drew information from multiple sources and was not cock-sure of being right. The second group (hedgehogs) took big bets by making positive affirmations confidently with no doubt in their mind at all.

When it is difficult to predict, it is perfectly fine to admit the difficulty. Because you are perceived as an expert, you are asked your view on subjects which you have no way of predicting. You go ahead and predict so as to maintain your self-image as an expert. What will the US dollar-INR exchange rate be? Will the RBI reduce interest rates? Will the market for my product be 1000 or 5000? Will the monsoon this year be good or bad? And so the predictions game continues.

The history of affirmative technology predictions is very sobering.

- In 1877, Western Union Company, USA, stated, 'The telephone has too many shortcomings to be considered as a means of communication and is inherently of no value to our company'.
- In 1894, Albert Michelson, eminent physicist said 'The more important fundamental laws and facts of the physical sciences have all been discovered and so firmly established that the possibility of their ever being supplanted is exceedingly remote.'
- In 1895, Lord Kelvin, President of the Royal Society said, 'Heavier-than-air flying machines are impossible.'
- In 1899, Charles Duell, Chairman of the US Patent Office, stated, 'Everything that can be invented has been invented.'
- In 1943, founder of IBM Thomas Watson said, 'I think there is a world market for computers of may be five computers.

Coincidences

'I can calculate the movement of the stars but not the madness of men,' wrote Sir Isaac Newton.

In a complex array of things, it is very difficult to predict because a small change can produce disproportionate effect, called the butterfly effect. Linearity is not the norm in the world, non-linearity is. Uncertainty is an ineradicable fact of existence. What follows is an array of unlikely examples to support the point that coincidences seem to determine more than what we might imagine.

In his delightful book, *Luck* (London, 2012), former England test cricketer Ed Smith enumerates a number of coincidences from history.

In the 1890s South African businessman Dada Abdulla requested lawyer Mohandas Gandhi to represent his legal case and to undertake a train journey from Pretoria to Pietermaritzburg.

Had Gandhi not been thrown out of the train, India may still be a colony.

On 28th June, 1914, the Austro-Hungarian Archduke, Franz Ferdinand, was being conducted in a procession through Sarajevo. Seven Bosnian-born Serbs had plotted to assassinate the Archduke to push their demand for a Greater Serbia. The first attempt on Ferdinand's life was assigned to Nedelijo Cabrinovic who botched it up. The cavalcade was cancelled and the Archduke's chauffeur sped away. One of the seven assassins, Gavrilo Princep, sat disconsolately at a meat shop to eat a Pljeskava, a popular meat patty in the Balkans. To his great surprise, the Archduke's driver had taken a wrong turn and was there—right in front of the meat shop—with the Archduke and his wife in the car. Princip quickly grabbed his revolver and fired just two bullets: one got the wife and the other the Archduke. The basis for the First World War was thus set.

When an apparently minor event snowballs into something major, it is called a *monkey bite effect*. Here is the story behind the expression. Alexander was the second son of King Constantine I of Greece. In 1917, on the assumption that Alexander would be an effective puppet king, the powers that be crowned Alexander as king; his father and elder brother were exiled. In 1919, King Alexander controversially married a commoner, thus creating a significant controversy. On 2nd October 1920, the king and his consort took a walk on the grounds of the Tatoi estate. A macaque monkey in the garden attacked the king's German shepherd dog. The king attempted to separate the dog and the monkey when another monkey approached Alexander and bit him. The king's wounds were cleaned, but not cauterised. After a fortnight the king died. The exiled father, King Constantine, returned to Greece. A war with Turkey followed and a quarter of a million people died.

On 22nd August 1931, John Scott-Ellis, a young Englishman, was taking his new Fiat around Munich for a spin. As he drove up Ludwigstrasse, he took a right turn into Briennerstrasse, but a pedestrian crossed the road. He was knocked down on one knee. Scott Ellis was reassured that he had not injured the pedestrian as the man picked himself up and walked away. Three years later, Scott-Ellis, now twenty-one years of age, sat at the box office at Residentz Theater. In the adjacent box sat the same man he had knocked down. The man recalled the incident but was 'quite charming for those few moments.' Later Scott-Ellis realized that he had knocked down Adolf Hitler.

On 13th December 1931, an English politician was knocked down on New York's Fifth Avenue. The car was driving at 35 mph, a speed enough to kill him. The veteran MP was fifty-seven years of age and was dragged several yards before being flung to one side. Churchill was rushed to Lenox Hill hospital and he survived.

In 1957, as the founder members of the EU met at Messina to hammer out the final details of the Treaty of Rome, the British sent a civil servant called Russel Breatherton. Leaving early he said, 'They won't agree to anything. If they agree to anything, they won't do it. If they do it, it won't work.' The EU did become a reality after that.

In 1988, Clyde Prestowitz wrote *Trading Places* (New York, 1988) and he totally ignored China and India because he worried that America and Japan were about to trade places. In 1990, Jacques Attali published a book *Millenium* (New York, 1990) in which he stated that the miracle of China and India integrating into the world trade was most unlikely. In *Head to Head* (New York, 1992), Lester Thurow dismissed China in two pages and never mentioned India because they would have no impact on the world economy in the first half of the twenty-first century.

The Berlin Wall would not have fallen on 9th November, 1989 if East German Guenter Schabowski, the spokesman of President Egon Krenz, had not bungled a press query about when free movement across the wall would be permitted. When he was asked 'when', he inadvertently responded 'immediately' instead of 'November 10th *under strict supervision*.'

George Bush asked Charles Wang casually in 1996 about who would win when he stood for re-election against Bill Clinton. He replied that Bill Clinton could not possibly win because never in American history had a left-handed, sitting President been re-elected. It was a correlation, not causation.

On 1st December 1955 in Montgomery, Alabama, if Rosa Parks had given up her bus seat quietly, Barrack Obama may not have become President of the USA.

Superstition

Two-time table-tennis Olympian, sports writer and broadcaster Matthew Syed has filled his book *Bounce* (New York, 2010) with many stories and statistics about sports and sportsmen.

Goran Ivanesevic became convinced that if he had to win a match, he had to duplicate his actions. He had to eat in the same restaurant, even watch the same TV programs. During Wimbledon tournaments, he had to watch the children's' program *Teletubbies* every morning.

The unfailingly courteous Rafael Nadal skipped the Royal appointment in Wimbledon 2010 because he had not met the queen on the day before. He had to follow his winning routine even if that meant missing meeting the queen.

South African cricketer Neil McKenzie became convinced that he would perform well only if he attached his spare cricket bats to the ceiling of the changing room using adhesive tape.

Baseball player Jim Ohms puts a coin in his jockstrap after every winning match. By the end of the season, opponents would hear the clang of the coins as Jim ran towards the base.

Australian rugby winger David Campese insisted that he sit next to the bus driver during the journey to every match.

When Venus Williams lost the 2008 French Open Tennis, she said it was due to: 'I didn't tie my laces right and I didn't bounce the ball five times and I didn't bring my shower sandals to the court with me.'

Superstition is what happens when we confuse randomness (which we cannot control) with causes (which we can control). Part of growing up is recognising the limitations of your willpower. Accepting that forces exist beyond your control is part of being a well-adjusted adult.

The allure of good luck

We like to believe that life is like serving in tennis, and this is pretty much encoded in your brain. You'd like to think that most of your life is controlled. Admitting the existence of luck demands the acknowledgement that some things are beyond our control, and the control-freak side of human nature is never going to accept such an uncomfortable state of affairs without a fight.

In 1928, bacteriologist Fleming made a chance discovery from an already discarded, contaminated petri-dish. The mould that had contaminated the experiment turned out to contain a powerful antibiotic, penicillin. It took another decade for it to become a wonder drug for the twentieth century.

James Watson, discoverer of the DNA structure, believed that life is like returning a tennis serve rather than like serving. He feels he had luck. It was a three horse race with him, American chemist Linus Pauling and Austrian biochemist Erwin Chargaff. Pauling and Chargaff were on the same boat after attending an international conference at Paris. They did not like each other so they did not talk throughout the journey. If they had talked, Pauling would have been the person to discover DNA.

Earned and unearned luck

It is, of course, true that it is not a good way to lead your life if you keep relying on good luck coming your way or bad luck not crossing your path. Deep and disabling faith in luck can be hugely debilitating. Yet the complete denial of luck too is worth a reconsideration.

When you have prepared for an event, and the event comes your way, you can justifiably feel that you have earned that luck. For instance you want that promotion to vice president; you slog hard and consistently deliver results as a general manager; you learn what there is to learn about the higher-level vice president's job; in other words, you develop yourself to a high state of preparedness. The current vice president retires and you get the job. You have deserved the promotion, it is an earned luck, QED.

A slightly different case. You have done all that is stated above. But so too has a colleague. It is clear to everyone that the promoted person will be one of you both. Some think you, and others think the other person. It is a close call. Three months before the current vice president retires, the other person dies in a car accident. You don't revel in his misfortune, but you become the beneficiary of unearned luck by becoming the single candidate for the bigger job. Unearned luck QED.

In my experience, luck matters and admitting that it matters, matters even more—call it unearned luck if you will. It is true that you can miss reaping the benefits of unearned luck, but the fact remains that there is something called unearned luck.

When I was posted to Jeddah in end 1990 as chairman, Unilever Arabia, war clouds were gathering over Saddam Hussein's belligerence with Kuwait. Many thought I was unlucky to be posted at such a time to what might become a war-ravaged geography. Indeed on the morning of 12th January 1991 when I reported at London for my formal induction, the US Congress passed a joint resolution authorising the use of military force to drive Iraq out of Kuwait. Operation Desert Storm had begun. Unilever director Chris Jemmett, my boss, welcomed me on that cold, bleary January day of 1991 with the cheerful words, 'Welcome, the war has begun.'

As I settled down to the tasks of the newly appointed chairman, travelling between London and Jeddah, the events of the war moved decisively. By 27th February, 1991, US Marines and Saudi Arabian troops entered Kuwait city and engaged in what came to be known as the battle of Medina Ridge. Within a few days, Kuwait accepted the UN ceasefire resolution. The war was over.

There was massive government spending after the war throughout the Gulf Cooperation Council states. The economy became buoyant and greatly helped me to establish Unilever's Arabian business on a sound footing. Of course there was earned luck insofar as Unilever had been preparing to invest in the geography for many years. But there was unearned luck insofar as the economic boom lifted Unilever's efforts with the rising tide. And I happened to be chairman…luck for me, and, of course, all my colleagues.

Here is another example from the field of sports. India was desperate to win some medals at the London Olympics in 2012. All eyes were set on Saina Nehwal who was playing great badminton. On 4th August, 2012, the eighth day of the London Olympics, India's badminton star, Saina Nehwal, competed with China's Wang Xin for the bronze medal. Left-handed Wang was seeded number 2 in the world at that time and, in a sense, had the psychological advantage to win. Wang won the first game 21-18. However in the last point of the game, Wang twisted her knee while smashing acrobatically from the baseline.

Since she had strained her knee, Wang received on-court treatment for her knee. At the beginning of the second game,

Wang winced and it became obvious that she was in great pain. Soon Wang conceded the match and shook hands with Saina with a wince. Saina Nehwal became the first Indian woman ever to win an Olympic bronze in badminton. Without any discredit to the top game played by Saina, it was surely a case of unearned luck.

Bad days or bad luck

Two Tata companies underwent extreme situations caused by factors of bad luck totally outside of their control. The episodes caused great stress to management and workers for extended periods of time. Since both have been prominent in the public domain, only brief references appear below in the book.

The state of Assam went through an ordeal during the late 1990s and early 2000s with internal unrest and separatist activities being rampant. The tea industry was caught into this maelstrom, just sheer luck of the draw. Tata Tea both experienced harrowing times, causing great grief and tension within the company management.

The tea industry in Assam was the largest employer of people. A separatist movement brewed in Assam from the 1980s onwards but the tea industry was left out of the consequences of the movement. Alarming events developed around 1989—manager of the Ledo Estate was hacked to death, a field clerk of Williamson Magor was shot dead, a Tata Tea employee was shot dead and in a high profile killing, the chairman of the Assam Frontier Tea Company was shot. Alarmed by the spate of killings, the Assam government set up a Plantation Security Force (PSF) to protect the estates. Neither could the PSF match the fire power of the terrorists nor could the Assam government pay for and sustain the PSF.

There was, in short, a complete breakdown of trust in Assam. The tea industry felt that it had to fend for itself. Many tea companies paid off the terrorists. Tata Tea refused to do so. The company started a medical assistance scheme for the benefit of the Assamese people. The scheme, like any scheme, could be misused in small ways.

Seven years later in 1997, a woman named Pranati Deka, along with her new-born baby, was arrested in Mumbai. She was the cultural secretary of the banned outfit ULFA (United Liberation Front for Assam). Tata Tea was accused of having borne the expenses of her hospitalisation at the Jaslok Hospital at Mumbai. There were many twists and turns, much accusation and tension. The powers that be in the State, it appeared, wanted to show the tea industry the trouble they could cause if they did not toe his line. Terror returned to Assam and it took several years to return to some degree of normalcy. It was a horrible time for the tea industry but an even worse time for Tata Tea. Huge bad luck!

On 26th November 2008, four terrorists entered the Taj Mahal Hotel, Mumbai and took over the hotel. What followed was three days of terror as the world watched the great hotel go up in flames. There were heart-stopping stories of guests and staff—of a couple about to celebrate their wedding, a British-Cypriot shipping magnate whose state-of-the-art yacht was docked in front of the hotel, and a young Taj employee who survived because of a stranger's phone call. The city of Mumbai was shocked, indeed the whole world was mesmerised with the huge bad luck faced by the hotel employees, the innocent people killed and the many injured. Call it bad days or bad luck, it was an experience of horrific proportions.

Jamshed Irani's trysts

I interviewed former Tata Sons director, Jamshed Irani, for this book. His narrative appears in these last chapters of the book. One of the subjects we both explored was Jamshed's idea of and acceptance of luck.

'Luck does not exist,' he said emphatically. 'You spin a coin for the cricket toss, then it is luck. But when you have prepared for an opportunity and your preparedness meets that opportunity, you grab it. Others may think it was luck, but I say, you prepared for it.'

As Jamshed talked about his early life and career, it became evident that there were coincidences that could be considered good luck or, at the very least, unearned luck. There were three unforeseen and unplanned interventions from a man whom he hardly knew at that point of time—JRD Tata.

Jamshed recollected his student days in Nagpur in the 1950s. His father had worked in Tata Empress Mills and so did his future father-in-law. On his own merit, Jamshed won a Tata scholarship to study geology and metallurgy in England. His family could not have afforded to send him on their own finances. In one sense, winning that scholarship marked the beginning of his personal association with the House of Tata.

He reminisced, 'There was a formidable lady who used to select the Tata scholars, grill them and also make sure that they stayed in contact. She would put up notes to JRD Tata. As I was finishing my studies in England, it seems that JRD had remarked that if ever this person wants to come back to India, ask him to first knock on the doors of Tata Iron and Steel Company (TISCO). That lady sent me the comment, stating that I should feel very proud that JRD had said what he had said...as he rarely did so.' A bit of unearned luck or a coincidence, I wondered.

Jamshed did want to return to India and he did knock on the doors of TISCO. He was interviewed by Mr JRD Tata and Mr Sumant Moolgaonkar, initially in Mumbai. Later the Director-in-charge, Mr Nanavati, travelled to Sheffield and interviewed the young Jamshed in his office in England. An offer was made and Jamshed joined Jamshedpur in 1968 in the research department.

As a safety net, he retained a lien on his job at British Steel for one year. He wanted to test how his professional life might shape up in TISCO.

The early period in Jamshedpur was not particularly enjoyable for Jamshed. He just did not enjoy the research job within his department. After several months of trying to find enjoyment in his job, he wrote to the company about his intention to return to his job in England. The bosses accepted his letter and Jamshed was all set to return.

And then another coincidence (or unearned luck?) happened. JRD was on an unplanned visit to Jamshedpur. He saw Jamshed along with a larger group of TISCO officers and enquired how 'the young man' was getting along. Jamshed was forthright in informing JRD that he was not enjoying the job and that he had decided to return to England. All that JRD said was, 'Oh,' and he walked away. On the day after JRD left Jamshedpur, three directors—Russi Mody, Nanavati and R.S. Pandey—summoned Jamshed to enquire why he was not enjoying his job. Upon listening to his reasons, they offered him an alternative role within the manufacturing department in the steel plant. This development must be attributed to JRD's intervention (unearned luck?). Jamshed felt he had met his challenge and started to enjoy his new role enormously, so much so that he started visualising his long term career ambition to reach the highest levels in TISCO.

Several years later, Jamshed was approached—without his seeking the opportunity—to join SAIL (Steel Authority of India Limited) as the Chairman. In those days, joining the public sector was considered a nationalistic thing to do. Jamshed mentioned the SAIL approach to Russi Mody, who promptly reported the matter to JRD. JRD's response was something like, 'If Jamshed even considers whether he wants to go to SAIL, then he must have his head examined because obviously he does not know the difference between Tata and SAIL!' Jamshed had anyway decided to stay at TISCO, but he counted this third intervention by JRD as a fortuitous coincidence (or unearned luck).

I asked Jamshed about a more recent coincidence or unearned luck. Through whatever process of turmoil there was at the time, he was appointed as the CEO of TISCO in 1991. His appointment coincided with the country's national economic crisis. Liberalisation and delicensing began with a bang under the Prime Ministership of Narasimha Rao and the Finance Ministership of Manmohan Singh. This unforeseen development gave Jamshed an unparalleled opportunity to reconstruct, renovate, modernise and downsize TISCO—all of which were badly needed moves. Had this development not occurred, Jamshed would have been yet another CEO of TISCO, who managed the government interface and steel price controls. Instead he could aspire to become—and he succeeded—the architect of setting TISCO on an entirely new and dynamic trajectory. Coincidence (or unearned luck?). 'Well, for sure, the liberalization was not influenced by me,' said Jamshed Irani wistfully.

11

Success and Fulfilment: The Sixth Lens

'Don't aim at success—the more you aim at it and make it a target, the more you are going to miss it. For success, like happiness, cannot be pursued; it must ensue, and it only does so as an unintended side-effect of one's dedication to a cause greater than oneself or as the by-product of one's surrender to a person other than oneself... Then, you will live to see that in the long run, success will follow you precisely because you had forgotten to think about it.'

Viktor Frenkl, *Man's Search for Meaning*

In the late 1800's, Swami Vivekananda went to Chicago to attend the Parliament of Religions. He became a very ardent and outspoken advocate of human values. One of the people he met in Chicago was John D. Rockefeller, who had made a great fortune in the booming oil business at that time. John D. Rockefeller was introduced to Swami Vivekananda by a friend. Madame Emma Calve, a French lady disciple narrated this episode to Madame Drinette Verdier, who has written about their meeting in her diary. That is my source.

The sparse and austere John D. Rockefeller visited Swamiji most likely out of curiosity rather than any urge to meet; Swamiji didn't even look up from his desk when Rockefeller entered. He continued to do his work. After a while, he looked up to John D. Rockefeller, who was not really being used to be treated like a common person. He took his seat and a conversation ensued. It became apparent to Swamiji that Rockefeller had lots of wealth.

Swamiji posed him a question, 'If you have <u>that much</u> more money than other people, do you think <u>that much</u> smarter than the other people?' John D. Rockefeller said, 'Of course'. If he wasn't a hundred times smarter, he wouldn't have a hundred times the money, would he? Swamiji left him with the thought that he may not be one hundred times smarter, he maybe just three times smarter. If he had made a hundred times more money by being three times smarter, then perhaps he was merely an instrument through which this money had to go back to somebody else. Why don't you think about it? And why don't you consider leaving some of your money for other people?

This sounded absolutely ridiculous to Rockefeller, and he departed with the polite statement that he had worked really hard to make his money. He had absolutely no intention of leaving it to other people. But curiously, three weeks later, he came back to see Swami Vivekananda, this time of his own accord. He threw on his table a piece of paper, by which he endowed a certain sum of money for some noble purpose. He asked a Swami Vivekananda, 'Are you happy now that I have done this?' Swamiji responded, 'Why should I be happy? You have to ask yourself the question whether you have left enough out of the total wealth that you have?'

It took another fifteen years after this episode until 1913 when John D. Rockefeller set up the Rockefeller Foundation, which has done an enormous amount of good work in society for the last several decades. Just before his death in 1937, he whispered to his nurses, 'Just raise me a bit higher.' In an instant, John Rockefeller departed, peacefully, at his home in Ormond

Beach, California. The bells in the steeple at his Union Baptist Church were tolled to mark his passing. During his life he had given away US $530 million to various educational, scientific and religious institutions, winning the right to be called the world's greatest philanthropist. It appears that he died embracing success and fulfilment.

Are all fulfilled people always successful? It would appear so, because they have defined success on their terms. Think of Swami Vivekananda or Mother Teresa or Baba Amte among famous people. Or, if I may point out, your dad, uncle or grandmother, who may not be well-known, but perhaps have done an immeasurable lot for your family, a central mission in their life. They probably were hugely fulfilled people—and they must be regarded as successful because of the fact that they achieved what they set out to achieve, not what others measured their success by.

What about the converse? Are all successful people always fulfilled? To start with, it is difficult to define what a successful person is. If a person is successful because the person accomplished what he or she set out to accomplish, then the answer is yes, the successful person stands fulfilled. However so often in life, you set out to achieve what other people expect you to achieve—power, pomp and prestige. In such cases the answer is less clear.

The characteristic of a fulfilled person is that he or she is at peace with the self, that he or she has tried his or her best possible in life. Now the person is happy, with no negative feelings or bitterness. It is natural to have regrets, but the person is clearly content with a glass for its fullness rather than unhappy with a glass for its emptiness. One must feel blessed to feel fulfilled.

Fulfilled people seem to always aim for a goal outside of themselves, they are not all about me and us!

Strong influence of childhood

Fulfilled people often refer to childhood influences as having had a particularly strong influence in shaping life's perspectives. When Nihal Kaviratne spoke to me about how he came to set up St Jude, he first referred to his childhood, and how he had absorbed his mother's strong association with charity. When Geeta spoke about raising funds for cancer, she first spoke about generosity as a value, inculcated in her by her grandparents.

I was interested to read what Ed Smith had to say in his book *What Sports Tells Us about Life* (London, 2009). To do a programme called 'Peak Performance' on UK Radio 3, Smith interviewed musicians about their life as performers, expecting some similarities with sportspeople: nerves, pressure, ambition, relentless training, et al. He did hear all of that, but he was surprised to hear a lot about childhood.

Some artistes recalled the exact circumstance when they stepped on to the stage for their first performance. One recalled how she was snubbed by a primary schoolteacher and desperately wanted to prove the teacher wrong. Another spoke of her sense of frustration that day-to-day living did not give her a chance for self-expression, so she pursued music.

It was the same with sportsmen. Jackie Stewart, three-time Formula One champion, admitted that 98 per cent of his effort came from the need to prove himself different from the failure he had been dubbed in his school.

And so it was when I had a conversation with Dr Jamshed Irani, former managing director of Tata Steel, and my colleague on the Tata Sons Board.

Recalling father

The person who had the greatest influence on Jamshed, though he didn't realise it at the time, was his father. In his father young Jamshed, an only son, perceived a passion for education. This was perhaps because his father himself had not had a chance for higher education. He had just about passed school and he had started working at the age of seventeen, when he joined Empress Mills, the textile company of Tata in Nagpur.

'My regret is that I could not thank my father enough whilst he was alive,' rued Jamshed wistfully. 'I have sat back to think that this is what I would have liked to have told him before he was taken away rather abruptly. He died within a few minutes of getting a heart attack. It was a lovely end for him but a great shock for the rest of us in the family.'

Jamshed recalled a characteristic that his father instilled in him. His family was not poor, but by no means was the family rich. His father used to keep quoting Shakespeare, 'Never a borrower nor a lender be' until the message was imprinted on to Jamshed's young brain. As he reflected later in life, it was meant to instil the thrift value in the youngster, not to expose him to Shakespearean literature. And his father succeeded.

'That message stayed with me throughout my career in Tata Steel and certainly when I was managing director,' said Jamshed. 'Sometimes I didn't want to go into projects where we had to borrow huge sums of money and I was even told that I was too conservative. My vision was to continue the reality that we were a modest but very rich company.'

Jamshed felt that in the circumstances of TISCO in those days of severe controls, he was always the one who wanted to cut every possible cost absolutely to the bone. I asked whether subordinates in the company and peers in the industry would likely have thought of him, when he was the chief executive, as a conservative leader rather than a Rambo guy who went after acquisitions. Jamshed is convinced that such an impression is more than likely and that one of the influences on his attitude was his father's advice.

'Very conservative? Yes, my father's influence, most definitely. I always told my managers that the bottom line was what we were after. The top one gives you a lot of publicity, your profile goes up but if that is not accompanied by an equivalent rise in the bottom line, we are in trouble.'

Another strong influence from childhood was the inculcation of godliness through religion. After performing his son's Navjot ceremony, every evening before dinner, Jamshed's father would insist that young Jamshed pray for about ten minutes. Jamshed admits that he did not understand anything about the prayers, but accepted his father's advice that this would give him serenity. In later years he concurred that it did give him serenity. Whenever there was something disturbing to him, he would pick up his prayer book and recite the same prayers that his father had taught him. He can't understand what he reads—the language is Zend-Avesta—but the act of praying gives him a feeling of serenity, that he has done something positive.

With a tinge of pride Jamshed recalls that his father rose to the second-most senior level in Empress Mills even though he didn't have a university education. He was very well-liked by colleagues and he was an enthusiastic sportsman. As the treasurer of the National Hockey Federation, his father managed the finances of the sports body while he worked alongside Naval Tata. There, too, his father was conservative with expenditure.

Jamshed has tried to do most things in his life according to his father's inspiration.

Coping with work stresses

The joining experiences in TISCO of Jamshed Irani have been touched upon in the earlier chapter. On the whole, reminiscing now, Jamshed feels that he has had a very pleasant and satisfying career. This did not mean that he did not face turmoil, self-doubt and turbulence. These are a normal part of anybody's career.

There was a great deal of rivalry among Tata chief executives in his early Tata days. Two episodes stayed in Jamshed's memory.

Tata Chemicals at one time required coke of small sizes, which TISCO called nut coke. This was actually being wasted in Jamshedpur because TISCO couldn't use it in its steel blast furnaces. Jamshed thought that nut coke could be supplied to Tata Chemicals, which could profitably use the material. Then TISCO boss Russi Mody disapproved of the idea. Finally, Tata Chemicals Chairman Darbari Seth accosted Jamshed in Bombay House and said, 'Look, if necessary, I'll raise it with JRD Tata; you must give us that material.' Without asking Mody, Jamshed, as the plant-in-charge of the time, started sending regular supplies of nut coke to Tata Chemicals.

There was another incident. TISCO was in need of some additional equity and it was not easy for the company to raise that money. Jamshed mentioned to Russi Mody that Tata Chemicals and Tata Tea, both under Seth's watch, appeared to have surplus funds at that moment of time. Why not TISCO ask those companies to invest a small amount in TISCO? Mody said, 'Jamshed, not one share will I sell to Darbari Seth; just forget that, not one share. We may be in difficulty but we will find our way out.'

In those days Tata leaders were not really working as a team. The way to becoming one cohesive group and working as a team was finally ushered in by Ratan Tata, who, in a quiet sort of way, made sure that all Tata companies moved in the same direction. Tata is now a far more congenial and unified team than what prevailed during the earlier decades of Jamshed's career. The exercise of unification was initiated by Ratan Tata in the 1990s.

Jamshed recounted the turbulent days when the succession of Russi Mody was being decided. Those eighteen months were quite unpleasant. Mody was obviously being misled by some of the people who were around him. Jamshed was convinced that it would be ethical to back the House of Tata when it became clear to him that Mody's aim was to take control of TISCO. Jamshed remembers that TISCO board meetings became a bit dysfunctional, even bitter, during those months. Mody was chairman of TISCO. JRD Tata, of course, remained on the board and he was a strong influence. Some non-executive directors—Keshub Mahindra, Nusli Wadi, Ratan Tata and Sam Palia among them—made sure that the 'Tata-ness' was maintained.

From Jamshed's point of view, JRD once more featured in a coincidence in his life. When he called on JRD to express his anguish, JRD said, 'Jamshed, you don't have to tell me anything. I know everything, I have heard about what is going on and I have faced this sort of situation many times in my career. I have always solved such problems and I will solve this also. You don't get disheartened.'

Turmoil and dilemma

Jamshed recalls the fateful date of November 26, 1991 when TISCO Chairman and Managing Director Russi Mody issued an organisational circular regarding top leadership changes without consulting the TISCO board. Russi appointed an additional MD and a joint MD to the board. He then proceeded on business to London. Directors like Deputy Chairman Ratan Tata and Noshir Soonawala wrote letters to Russi and pointed out that the appointments could be made only after a board discussion and approval.

Russi Mody returned from London via Delhi, where, to the surprise of many, he lobbied the finance minister to instruct the government-led financial institutions to vote against Tata. JRD and Ratan Tata also visited Delhi to explain the Tata point of view.

Over the next few months JRD started to speak of the need for a retirement policy, which was finally presented to the TISCO board in December 1992. Ten minutes into JRD's talk, Mody closed his papers and announced that the meeting was over. He walked out. The directors of Tata Steel were a bit aghast at what had happened. At that time Nani Palkhivala said, 'We must have somebody in the chair whilst the meeting goes on; we must do this properly.' So Ratan Tata took the chair. The retirement policy of seventy-five years was proposed and accepted unanimously.

The board had another meeting within six weeks, on January 3, 1993. Mody's position as chairman of the board was terminated. A lot of negative publicity followed. Mody settled down in Calcutta, where he started his own trading company.

Jamshed recounted, 'I felt very sorry because Russi Mody had helped me in my earlier days. I did not find peace when my relationship was disturbed in this sudden manner. Through a mutual friend in Calcutta, I was encouraged to connect with Russi. Russi desired a particular Calcutta house which he wanted as a settlement. He stayed in this house right till his end. In this manner Russi Mody's parting was settled.

'Several years later, a mutual friend suggested that I go and see Russi, because sometimes he would mention me and my wife, Daisy, in his conversations. Daisy was very hesitant, but we both went and met him for breakfast. It was important for both of us to patch up our relationship with Russi, if at all we could. To our delight, Russi acted as if the previous five or seven years had not occurred. The conversation was just like the old days. I felt as if a great load had been taken off my chest. I continued meeting him till the time that he died, following his 96th birthday. Neither of us had recriminations built up. The fight, so to speak, was forgotten. It is the only way to live a sane life out of all the turbulence that a career throws your way.'

Jamshed often uses the expression Tata-ness. He feels that

the future holds the danger of our work culture losing its Tataness, that special feeling which pulls Tata colleagues together. Every time Jamshed would meet a new recruit, (including when I joined in 1998) he would invite the person to Jamshedpur and impress upon him to read a copy of the book, *The Creation of Wealth* (Bombay, 1981) by Russi Lala. That book covered Tataness very well, something which Jamshed would very much like to see flourishing in the future as well.

Tandoori chicken at an Udipi restaurant

Bihar once had a reputation for changing chief ministers every few months. Some were good, some were terrible. Lalu Prasad was a student leader before becoming the state's chief minister, almost the same time that Jamshed became TISCO's managing director. And Lalu started making statements that South Bihar is too far away from Patna, and would publicly posture, 'Who is Tata anyway?'

It was not a negative feeling; it was the absence of anything positive. A senior director in Bombay House advised Jamshed, 'Chief ministers in Bihar change every few months. You just ride out this phase and in a few months there will be another chief minister.' Jamshed didn't take that advice; just as well because between him and his wife Lalu Prasad ran Bihar for seventeen years.

Recounted Jamshed, 'I sought a meeting. I was ushered into a room which was full of people, secretaries, and ministers; I just stood in a corner. Lalu asked all the people to leave the room and there was just the two of us left in the room. I told him in my broken Hindi that my steel company and the progress of Bihar went hand-in-hand. That had been how it was for almost one hundred years. After we, as individuals, go away from our current roles, the institutions hopefully will carry on. So let's have a clear understanding. He said okay.

'My situation is that I can't give new people any jobs at TISCO, because we are in manpower reduction mode. However, any honest effort that benefits the community will receive our support.'

That was the end of the interview. Jamshed is unsure what precisely Lalu took away as a message. But he is categorical that Lalu never made an improper request of TISCO, ever. Previous ministers used to keep on sending chits and making phone calls, almost every day. But Lalu never did that. Jamshed dealt with Lalu with openness. Jamshed recalled a severe winter when TISCO sent blankets with the logo, TMH, for the Tata Main Hospital. Looked at from the other side, it read HMT. The word in Patna was that HMT was giving all these away. Finally TISCO devised a clearer logo.

On one occasion Lalu came to Jamshedpur. He saw TISCO's earth-moving equipment inside the plant. He was least interested in steelmaking; he wanted to borrow that equipment to clean up Patna. Jamshed figured that once given the equipment might never come back. However, on the condition that it would be only for two weeks, TISCO could agree. But TISCO would send its own mechanics and drivers, who were familiar with the equipment. Lalu concurred. TISCO sent the equipment and, exactly after a fortnight, the equipment came back; no reminders, nothing. Based on his dealings with Lalu, Jamshed had high praise for him as a man of his word.

Lalu used to tell his civil servants, police and other officials who came to Jamshedpur not to expect any concessions from Tata. Lalu's is favourite expression was this: 'You cannot go to an Udipi restaurant and ask for *tandoori chicken*; It is not on their menu.'

Every time Lalu had any problem of a social nature, TISCO would help. So he was happy. Whenever TISCO gave help, the company did not seek credit. During summertime, when the tanks dried up, TISCO would drill wells but the government could take the credit. Lalu would go around saying that his government had built fifteen tube wells. And TISCO would have helped the community without compromising the Tata principles.

Avoiding the bribing trap

A particular ferrochrome mine in Orissa was due for renewal. Everybody cleared it at the Orissa state level, and the papers went to Delhi. Jamshed followed to Delhi for a final courtesy meeting with the minister concerned. He had been given the impression that everything was cleared and his was a courtesy visit. But someone wanted Rs 4 crore.

The mine had been given to TISCO in the 1950s. In those days there was very little demand for chrome. The small quantity of chrome consumed in those days by India was being imported. So it became uneconomic for TISCO to invest and develop the mines. But the mine deposits were of a high quality, a rather distinctive ore with low iron content.

South African and other world mines have chrome with high iron content. When you purify the iron, it is not easy to separate iron from chrome and you end up with ferrochrome, which is chrome with high iron content. You don't get pure chrome with low iron content, which is required in making stainless steel and special metals. TISCO had access to low-iron chrome ore. However, the development of the mine was limited by small demand.

When the time for renewal came in the 1980s, Biju Patnaik was the Orissa chief minister. He offered support for TISCO's lease extension if the company would take over a public-sector, loss-making ferrochrome plant. Russi Mody readily agreed. TISCO worked out a price of Rs 156 crores, higher than the book value of the facility. This would cement the company's relationships with

Orissa and also give it continued access to quality ferrochrome mines. Patnaik had made up his mind and did not waver.

The papers for renewal travelled to the centre. One day Jamshed got a call to visit Delhi and meet the minister. He met the minister and he too said everything was fine. The minister had an assistant.

Perhaps the assistant decided to make some money by demanding Rs 4 crore. Jamshed regretted that TISCO could not pay such money. Soon someone changed the law. A commission was appointed, but the commission never visited the mine. Unbelievably, the law was changed to make it impossible for TISCO to retain the mine. Finally TISCO was asked to give up a part of the mine. TISCO gave up the part having 'less rich ore' but not without battling the matter in the courts. TISCO must have spent Rs 40 crore on the legal effort, but preferred to do so rather than giving a bribe of Rs 4 crore.

Some months later, the papers reported that the minister's assistant was caught red-handed in another case and put behind bars.

Balancing work and family

On the subject of peace of mind, it is just part of a day's work in a career that unsettling things happen: you don't get along with the boss, somebody is unreasonable, somebody makes unfair demands and it creates turmoil in your mind. How does a person cope? Furthermore, when a person is living in a campus city, the line of demarcation between office and home life can blur easily. And the consequences can be quite severe.

Jamshed recognised this possibility and planned assiduously to separate work and family. He would not carry work home and he absolutely refused to do office work at home. Anyone from my organisation who wanted to discuss office matters could come to his office during office hours. Once Jamshed returned home at 7 pm, he would lock up his briefcase. He would spend time with his children. As far as possible, every night the five of them—Jamshed, Daisy and the three children—would drive around town. His excuse was that he wanted to see what the goings-on in the town were. But in reality it was a very private drive. The family would have some ice cream or *chana bhatura*, play some games or together discover a new route to another venue in the city, just the kind of trivial things we all do within families and which make early life so memorable for children.

'In a way it helped me also because I could see what the town was like and if there were any areas where it required maintenance or attention,' recalled Jamshed. People knew that I was going around town, not as a watchdog but just for relaxation.'

Once the chief minister of Bihar burst into his house; on other occasions local tribal leaders would stop by with issues. Jamshed was always very polite. As soon as they started talking about work, Jamshed would offer to see them the next morning. And no one took umbrage.

Jamshed learnt about not mixing work and family from his experience in the United Kingdom. During his first few years in Jamshedpur he observed the blurring of the two and he did not want it that way. Just as an example, he had noticed that the general manager of a particular time was fond of movies. So he would go to the club to see movies. He would extend the interval breaks as all the superintendents would gather around him and try to impress him. Jamshed would never join that group. Sometimes colleagues and friends would be curious and suggest that he also join the chat group. For Jamshed it was a clear no-no.

'When I come home, that's the end of the plant for me. I would sometimes get a call about some issue or problem. I always told the caller, 'You've got the responsibility; go and settle it.' I never interfered with the job and people soon realised that they could not make me do something which was the responsibility of a person lower down. If you don't give that person the responsibility you can change him, but I would not do his job.' The image of Jamshed in the city was of a very fast decision maker. Once he decided he would not interfere with the implementation.

Dr Jitu Singh, the human resources chief, would occasionally talk to his closest colleagues to elicit a feedback on Jamshed. Where decision making was concerned, these colleagues were unanimous in scoring Jamshed high. But Dr Singh would receive comments about Jamshed's lack of sociability, for which he received low scores. The colleagues would appreciate his wife Daisy's contribution. So he never interfered with whatever Daisy was doing. He was quite confident that she would handle the social part very well.

One of the things about the Anglo-Saxon work culture is that they see the world in black and white. When they see something that's grey they will soon endeavour to put it into either the black or the white box and then get ahead. We Indians are socially and culturally wired to deal with ambiguity. In this respect, people very early realised that Jamshed was a bit Anglo-Saxon. He would divide things into black and white. If there was something wrong he would tell people to their face, never in a group but separately and privately. He would never say something just to please a person or to win and score a point, and that applied to the lowest colleague right up to JRD Tata.

Jamshed recounted a frank chat with the redoubtable JRD: 'JRD Tata used to keep telling me. 'What do we do; we have an old plant.' My good friend Firoze Tarapore was the chief engineer at the time. Firoze asked where the money was to do any upgrading. He used to joke that he had made as many plans to modernise TISCO as the years in his life, but the management always turned these down on the grounds of having no money.

'One day in the early 1980s, I told JRD: 'Unless we modernise this plant, we are gone. Government plants are coming up which are newer and better than TISCO's; this old warhorse cannot keep on racing against thoroughbreds. You and I may well be soon standing at the gates of TISCO to sell tickets to see this steel museum.' Luckily the circumstances in India changed and we started modernising. Within ten years we had the most modern plant, not only in India but I believe in the world, because the money was flowing in. By that time we tightened our manpower, halving it from almost 80,000 to 40,000.'

Fire in the factory

Jamshed recounted the story of March 3, 1989. 'It was the most regretful day of my life in TISCO. That fire during the Founder's Day procession occurred. We didn't have proper tents and my children were there. People were congested into one area and the fire started in one corner. I could see the fire starting. When I saw Daisy and the two girls moving out, there was a selfish relief for me.

'Then I and K.C. Mehra went in there and started pulling out people. There had been a stampede and we were trying to get people out of this. Both of us got singed on the face. We lost sixty people that day; it was agony for all of us. All we could do was to financially help and settle the families of the victims. I was very happy to get the wise advice of TISCO director L.P. Singh, who had been the Bihar chief secretary earlier. He advised the company to make a generous offer to start with and not wait for the lawyers to add complexity. We even sent patients to London and Paris for curing of the burn scars. Fali Nariman fought that case for TISCO without charging a single rupee, an act of great generosity at a time of tragedy.'

Reflecting pensively

Jamshed continued: 'Now when I look back, three years into retirement, I realise that I have achieved a certain level of serenity. I've always told all those near me that yes, we wish each other well on our birthdays, and we say good health for your future success and your job. But what I would like to add is peace of mind. I think peace of mind is as important as good health; it gives a person the feeling of having done something, of fulfilment. I worked to my limit and now I thank God for peace of mind.

'I feel contented in Jamshedpur. We have a lovely house. I am well taken care of financially. My children have had excellent education. Daisy and I are now indulgent with regard to travelling and seeing places. We have some good friends. We have a hospital to look after us in our old age and I feel much fulfilled.

'This characteristic of being able to separate office and house made me into a rather disciplined or self-assured sort of person. In my experience the type of office problem that bothers people is about, for example, the guy who is gossiping or buttering up the boss. Will he get one over me? Is the boss upset with me about something?

'People have told me, "You have such a good grip on Jamshedpur. Why do you not stand for elections?" I said elections and politics are not my cup of tea. I will do what is known, the right thing. I will follow the law, even if I think the law is unfriendly, like with mining. I will follow it but I will do everything possible to see that it is changed. Once it is changed then I am happy. If it is not changed we will follow the old law.

'A last few thoughts on rectitude and exemplary behaviour. Whenever I've taken actions on ethical grounds, I have also given a message. I need to emphasize that you cannot do this and get away with it in TISCO. On one occasion in a senior level succession planning, there was a very strong candidate. The entire selection committee was for him. But he had one weakness, and I strongly felt that this weakness was a character deficiency that a leader could not get away with. I blocked that person.'

People who are happy tend to keep and nurture relationships. Call it 'family' for lack of a better word, but it could be a school or college batch, it could be a cohort group in the company, it could be your family. Jamshed attached a great deal of importance to this aspect. Once every year he invites all the retired people who were his colleagues—a list of 40-50—for lunch on a Sunday to his house. In this way Jamshed keeps in touch with former colleagues.

Jamshed is acutely conscious that many people in Jamshedpur quietly help to make his and his family's life comfortable. They are among those invited for the annual lunch. Jamshed and Daisy give them a Parsi meal. In this way they keep building up the team spirit in Jamshedpur. (Jamshed and Daisy also entertain another group—orphans from the streets at Diwali and other special occasions.

Living life your way

This last story, indeed all of the stories in this book, suggests that each person has to live his or her life in his or her own way. The choice of that way is determined by the view he or she takes through the six lenses. When all that has been done and life has been lived out, to feel fulfilled is a privileged gift.

These sentiments were so evocatively captured by Frank Sinatra in his wonderful song.

My Way:

'And now, the end is near; and so I face my the final curtain,
My friend, I'll say it clear; I'll state my case, of which I'm certain.

*I've lived a life that's full. I've travelled each and ev'ry highway;
And more, much more than this, I did it my way.*

*Regrets, I've had a few; but then again, too few to mention.
I did what I had to do, and saw it through without exemption.
I planned each charted course; each careful step along the high way,
And more, much more than this, I did it my way.*

*Yes, there were times, I'm sure you knew, when I bit off more than I could chew.
But through it all, when there was doubt, I ate it up and spit it out.
I faced it all and I stood tall; and did it my way.*

*I've loved, I've laughed and cried. I've had my fill; my share of losing.
And now, as tears subside, I find it all so amusing
To think I did all that; and may I say, not in a shy way.
For what is a man, what has he got? If not himself, then he has naught.
To say the things he truly feels; and not the words of one who kneels.
The record shows I took the blows-and did it my way.
Yes, it was my way.'*

12

My Ideas Bank

I have been inspired by ideas from several books and publications in the course of writing this book. Here is a listing of some of them, though I feel sure that there would be many more.

1. *Authentic Leadership: Rediscovering the Secrets to Creating Lasting Value,* Bill George, San Francisco, 2003.
2. *The Marshmallow Test: Mastering Self-Control,* Walter Mischel, New York, 2014.
3. *The Progress Principle: Using Small Wins to Ignite Joy, Engagement, and Creativity at Work,* Teresa Amabile and Steven Kramer, Boston, 2011.
4. *Why Should Anyone Be Led by You?: What It Takes to be an Authentic Leader,* Rob Goffee and Gareth Jones, Boston, 2006.
5. *Creating the Good Life: Applying Aristotle's Wisdom to Find Meaning and Happiness,* James O'Toole, Emmaus, 2005.
6. *Man's Search for Meaning,* Viktor Frankl, Boston, 2008.
7. *Finding a Purpose in Life,* Russi Lala, New Delhi, 2009.
8. *The Courage to Act: 5 Factors of Courage to Transform Business,* Merom Klein and Rod Napier, Palo Alto, 2004.
9. *Trust: From Aristotle to Enron,* Kieron O' Hara, Cambridge, 2004.
10. *The Speed of Trust: The One Thing That Changes Everything,* Stephen Covey, New York, 2006.

11. *Purpose: The Starting Point of Great Companies*, Nikos Mourkogiannis, New York, 2006.
12. *Integrity: The Courage to Meet the Demands of Reality*, Henry Cloud, New York, 2006.
13. *Happiness: A History*, Darrin McMahon, New York, 2006.
14. *The Culture Map: Breaking through the Invisible Boundaries of Global Business*, Erin Meyer, New York, 2014.
15. *Trust: A History*, Geoffrey Hosking, Oxford, 2014.
16. *Trust: The One Thing That Makes or Breaks a Leader*, Les Csorba, Nashville, 2004.
17. *Trustbuilding: An Honest Conversation on Race, Reconciliation, and Responsibility*, Rob Corcoran, Charlottesville, 2010.
18. *Future Babble: Why Pundits are Hedgehogs and Foxes Know Best*, Daniel Gardner, New York, 2011.
19. *Luck: What It Means and Why It Matters*, Ed Smith, London, 2012.
20. *Bounce: Mozart, Federer, Picasso, Beckham, and the Science of Success*, Matthew Syed, New York, 2010.

Acknowledgements

I am deeply grateful to the three protagonists whose life stories appear in this book: Nihal Kaviratne, Geeta and Jamshed Irani. Each of them spent several hours talking to me, later reviewing my drafts and clarifying aspects within the context of this book. This trio form the PLU (people like us) part of the book, arising from the view that everybody's life is a story, the story is worth telling to others and the lessons that emerge are worth pondering about by the reader. Thanks a lot to each of them.

My subject could have made this book into a heavy and philosophical one. However I was keen to make it anecdotal and interesting. It became an incredibly difficult task. I had to rely on critical reviewers who would find it worthwhile to plough through the manuscript and offer their views, howsoever harsh they would be. These reviews caused me to write, rework, rework again and rework yet again. Thanks to Rajashekaran Nair, Pradipta Mahapatra, Christabelle Noronha, Sudha Raghavendran and my dear wife. I would also like to thank Bhairavi Sanghi for her valuable direction on the cover design.

If Ritu Vajpeyi-Mohan was not the nag that she progressively became as this manuscript evolved, this book would not have become what it has. The positives are entirely due to her nagging; the negatives are entirely to my account. The Rupa cover design team, the edit team and the production team have all been incredibly pro-active. A big thank you to the Rupa team.

Index

Abdulla, Dada, 65, 162, *see also* Gandhi, Mahatma
Adiga, Aravind, 26
'aha' moment, 64
Aitken, Richard L., 89
Albania, 47
American geopolitics, 128
Amte, Baba, 176
Anand, Bal, 39–40
Anglo-Saxon work culture, 188
Anna Karenina, 116
St Anthony, 39
Apoorva, 46
APV, *see* Venkateshwaran, A.P.
Aristotle, 74, 77
Arjuna, 67, 69, 72
art-based therapy and crafts, 39
ashrams of life, 74–5
Assam Frontier Tea Company, 169
assumptions, 61–2
authenticity, 62, 66–7, 94, 98, 100–2, 110, 139
   apostles of, 102
   aspects of, 101
   associate, 100
   common sense and self-awareness, 102
   consultants, 102
   deep personal and professional relationships, 102
   how we think of, 101–3
   learning from muddle of real life, 102
   mantra, 110–12
   self transforms, 110
   universal, 110
Awami League, 130

Badrinath, S., 80
Bahadur, Rajesh, 32, 50
Balancing work and family, 186–9
Bangladesh, 128–9
Bardeen, John, 86
Barret, Emma, 91
Bassein, 66
BDD *chawls*, 44, 46
Being There (movie), 52
Bengal Congress (1938), 97

Bhagavad Gita, 70, 149, 155
Bhat, Harish, 112
Bhishma, 67–8, 72–3
Black Scholes formula, 158
Blair, Tony, 95
Blood, Archer, 128, 130–2
Bolshevik revolution (1917), 141
Bolshevik Russia, 140–2
Bonner, James, 160
Book of Ruth, 70
Bose, Subhas Chandra, 95, 116, 136
Bounce, 165
Brahmins, 35, 47
Brailsford, H.N., 160
Brattain, Walter, 86
Breatherton, Russel, 164
bribing trap, avoiding, 185–6
British Petroleum (BP), 106
Brown, Brene, 11
Browne, Lord, 106–9
Bucher, General Roy, 119–24
Bukharin, Nikolai, 141
Butcher, Scott, 129

Cabinet Secretary Looks Back, A, 117
Cabrol, Natalie, 92
Calve, Madame Emma, 174
Campese, David, 165
Canada's Algonquin Park, 91
Cancer Patients' Association, 150
Cariappa, Lt Gen KM, 122

Carlsen, Captain, 98
Carroll, Joseph, 22
caste and religion, 47–8
Catholic Church, 47
celebrity stories, 5
certainty of uncertainty, 76
Chattopadhyaya, Kshitij Prasad, 96
Chaudhuri, Maj. Gen, 122
childhood, strong influence, 177
chip revolution, 86
Chitnis, Gajanand, 6
Chitnis, Leela, 6
Choksi, R.D., 34
Christensen, Clayton, 56–7
Christianity, 69
Christian-Muslim relations, 85
circles of interest, 75
Clark, John Bates, 159
Clinton, Bill, 165
conflict resolution, model, 143
coping with work stresses, 179–81
corporate governance, 104
Courage to Act, The, 114
Courage, 62, 113–14, 118
  charisma of, 67–8
  constituents, 115
  displays of ambition, boldness, 113
  King Sejong, 114–16
  leadership courage, 118–19
  is like beauty, 113

INDEX

non-financial principle, 124
Ravana, 124
Richard Nixon, 128
R.K. Talwar, 132
Sanjay Gandhi, 132
Vibhishana, 124
Father Victor, 84–5
Covey, Stephen, 101
Creation of Wealth, The, 183
Cyclone Bhola, 129

Daily Express, 98
D-day of voting, 2
de Bonhome, Father Jacques, 12, 20–1, 24
Deewaar (movie), 13
delaying gratification, 34
Deshmukh, B.G., 117
Diwanji, Jai, 46
Diwanji, Shishir, 46
Draupadi, 67–9
Druckerman, Pamela, 6
Duell, Charles, 162

East Bengal, *see* Bangladesh
easy-to-forget relationships, 8
Ehrlich, Paul, 160
Ekman, Paul, 59
Elimelech, 70
Elizabeth, Queen, 107
Elmhurst, Sir Thomas, 122
emotional and psychological life, 13
emotional flowering, 54

emotional well-being, 76
emotions, 56, 59, 151–2
Enron, scandals at, 109
eureka, 5

Fairchild Semiconductors, 86
Famine 1975, 160
Federer, Roger, 38, 64
Force Majeure (movie), 74
Ford, 87–9
 patent infringement, 88–9
Dr Fox Effect, 18–19
Fox, Myron L., 17–19
fulfillment seeking, 76–7
fund raising for charity, 145
Future Babble, 159

Gallup, 144
Gandhi, Feroze, 132
Gandhi, Indira, 129, 132–3
 emergency declaration, 133
 arm-twisting of nationalised banks, 133
Gandhi, Mahatma (Mohandas Karamchand Gandhi), 61, 71–2, 93, 95–7, 136, 162
Gandhi, Rajiv, 117–8, 145
Gandhi, Sanjay, 132–4
Gandhi-Irwin pact, 95
Gardner, Dan, 159
gathering and scattering, 74–5
gathering phase, 26
Geeta, 6, 145–55, 177
George Bush II, 95

George, V.A., 134
GlaxoSmithKline, 99
Glover, Jonathan, 27
Goethals Indian Library, 85
Grove, Andrew, 108
Grove, Andy, 86
Guardian, The, 74
Gulf Cooperation Council, 168
Gupta, Ravi, 149, 154

Hangeul, 115
Harijans, 47
Head to Head, 164
Hindustan Lever, 21–2, 28, 36
Hoffman, Donald, 23–4
How Will You Measure Your Life, 57
Human Knowledge Bank, 73
human quality, 73–4
humanity, 47–8
Huq, Fazlul, 97
Hussain, Ishaat, 112
Hussein, Saddam, 167
Huxley, Thomas, 23
Hyderabad police action, 119–24

Ibarra, Herminia, 94
IIT Sports Meet, 2
India Today, 117
An Indian Pilgrim, 96
Indian Struggle, The, 96
instrument of accession, 120
Intel Trinity, The, 86
Intel, 86, 108

intellectual binocularity, 27
Irani, Jamshed, 6, 111, 157, 170–3, 177, 179
Irish Parliamentary Party, 142
Irwin, Viceroy, 96
Isay, David Avram, 9
Islam, 31, 69, 85, 120
issue-based differences, 143
Ittehad (MIM), 120–1, 124
Ivanesevic, Goran, 165

Jesuit renunciation, 21
St Jude, 28, 38–9, 42–3, 45, 47–8, 52, 54, 145, 177

Kahurangi National Park, 90
Karna, 68–9
Kaviratne Place, 29
Kaviratne, Nihal, 6, 14, 27–8, 38, 56, 60, 75, 92, 145, 177
  amateur dramatics interests, 34
  Brahmin influence, 31
  career, 36
  childhood, 28–33
  delaying gratification habit, 34
  entertainment and travel, 41
  family, 27, 29–30
  holidays, 41
  Mallika (daughter), 36–7
  mannerism, 28
  melange of religions, 31
  raised with Western

influences, 27
  sense of self-control, 33
  Shyama (wife), 35
  vegetarian roots, 31
Kay, John, 158
Kearns, Bob, 87, 89
Keltner, Dacher, 59
Kelvin, Lord, 162
Khan, Mahmud Nawaz, 120
Khan, Yahya, 129
Killgore, Andrew, 129
Kirov, Sergei, 141
Kissinger, Henry, 129
Klein, Merom, 114
knowledge of philosophy, 62
Kohli, Sarla, 150, 154
Korean alphabet, see Hangeul
Krenz, Egon, 164
Krishna, Lord, 67-8, 70, 72
Kung San (African Kalahari), 137
Kunti, 68
Kurosawa, Akira, 8

Lala, Russi, 80, 92, 183
Lalu Prasad, 183
Laski, Harold, 10
Lehman Brothers, 158
Lever, Hesketh, 80
London Olympics, 168
Long Term Capital Management, 158
longstanding relationships, importance of, 49-52

Loungani, Prakash, 160
luck, 62, 71, 156, 158, 163, 171
  allure of good luck, 166-7
  bad days or bad luck, 169
  as a belief, 158-9
  coincidences, 157, 162-5
  earned and unearned, 167
  faith in experts, 159-60
  fox and the hedgehog, 161-2
  frailty of predictions, 159-61
  lure of luck, 69-71
  moods produced by luck, 157
  predictions, 157
  superstition, 165-6
  superstitions, 157
Lux soap (advertisement), 7

Mahabharata, 67-9
Mahindra, Keshub, 181
Malinowsky, Bronislaw, 137
Mallika, 27, 36-7, 46, 48-9, 51
Malone, Michael, 86
Management Today, 107
Manchester Guardian, 160
Mandela, Nelson, 93
Marquis, Sarah, 90-1
Martin, Paul, 91
Mathematical Game Theory, 17-18
McKenzie, Neil, 165
Meade, James, 161
Mehra, K.C., 189
Menon, V.K. Krishna, 82, 122

Menuhin, Yehudi, 38
Michelson, Albert, 162
Millenium, 164
mind-sets, 61–2
Modi, Narendra, 95
Mody, Russi, 173, 180–2, 185
monkey bite effect, 163
Montgomery General Hospital, 88
Moolgaonkar, Sumant, 171
Moore, Gordon, 86
Mother Teresa, 47–8, 176
Mountbatten, Lord, 120–1, 123
Muhammad, 65
Mukherjee, Rudrangshu, 95, 97
Murthy, Yogesh, 26
Muslim-Christian relations, 85

Nadal, Rafael, 165
Naipaul, V.S., 161
Nanavati, Kawas Manekshaw, 82–3
Nanavati, Mr, 172
Napier, Rod, 114
Napoleon, 156
Nariman, Fali, 189
National Hockey Federation, 179
Nehru and Bose: Parallel Lives, 95
Nehru, B.K., 10
Nehru, Jawaharlal, 95, 97, 122–3, 128, 132
Nehru-Gandhi family, 82
Nehwal, Saina, 168–9

Neitz, Jay, 22
Netralaya, Shankar, 80
New York Times, The, 90
Newton, Sir Isaac, 162
Niazi, A.A.K., 130
Nixon, Richard, 128–31
Noyce, Robert, 86

Ohms, Jim, 165
Operation Polo, 121, 123–4

Paddock, Paul, 160
Palia, Sam, 181
Palkhivala, Nani, 182
Pandey, R.S., 172
Panthea, 80
Parable of the Sadhu, The, 63
Parekh, Ramnik, 21
Parliament of Religions, 174
Parnell, Charles Stewart, 142
Patel, Vallabhbhai, 119–24
Pauling, Linus, 166
Pawar, Narayan Rao, 121
Pendse, Dilip, 111
people-centred fundraiser, 155
person like us (PLU), 4–6, 56
personal odyssey, 92–3
personal standard of conduct, 61
Plantation Security Force (PSF), 169
Population Bomb, The, 160
positive life, 63–4
princely states, 35, 120

Princep, Gavrilo, 163
Prishvin, Mikhail, 142
professional fund-raising consultants, 146
professionalism, 57
Purpose, 79
quest for happiness, 77–8

Raghavan, R.V., 15
Sri Rama, 66–7, 100, 124–5, 127
Ramanuja, Saint, 70
Ramayana, 101, 124, 127
Rao, Narasimha, 173
Rashomon (Japanese film), 8
Razwi, Qasim, 120–1
Regardie, 87
Rehman, Sheikh Mujibur, 130
Ribeiro, Julio, 44
Rockefeller Foundation, 80, 175
Rockefeller, John D., 80, 174–5
Roman Catholics, 142
Rovshen, Nilima, 154
Royal Bank of Scotland, 99
Royal Society, 162
Rub-al-Khali, 91

Sadhana School, 149–51
SAIL (Steel Authority of India Limited), 172
SBI Act, 134
scattering phase, 26
Scott-Ellis, John, 163
secret of success, 71–3

Securities Exchange Board of India (SEBI), 103–6
Sejong, King, 114–16
  invention of alphabet (Hangeul), 115
  social and economic reforms, 115
self-designed blend, 83–4
separatist movement, 169
Seth, Darbari, 180
Shockley Transistor Laboratories, 86
Shockley, William, 85–7
Shoshone people, 137–8
Shyama, 27, 30, 34–6, 39–41, 46, 60
Sinatra, Frank, 191
Singh, Baldev, 122
Singh, Jitu, 188
Singh, L.P., 189
Singh, Manmohan, 173
Sitaramayya, Pattabhi, 97
social traps, 140
Soonawala, Noshir, 111, 181
Sophia School for Special Children, 146
South Asia, policies in, 128
Speke, John Hanning, 92
spiral of silence, 106–10
Stalin, Joseph, 141
Standstill Agreement, 120
Storycorps, 9
stroboscopic effects, 21
Study of History, A, 160

success and fulfilment, 14–15
Suryadharna, Asikin, 53
Sutaputra, *see* Karna
Syed, Matthew, 165

Taj Mahal Hotel, 65
  terrorists attack, 170
Talwar amendment, 134
Talwar, R.K., 132–3
Tarapore, Firoze, 188
taste receptors, 22
Tata Finance, 111–2
Tata Iron and Steel Company (TISCO), 171
Tata Log, 112
Tata Medical Centre, 47, 145, 151
Tata Memorial Centre, 43
Tata Memorial Hospital, 153
Tata Tea, 169–70, 180
Tata, JRD, 33, 80, 110, 138, 171–2, 180–1, 188
Tata, Ratan, 110–2, 180–2
Tata-ness, 181
Taylor, A.J.P., 160
theory of life, 56–9
Thesiger, Wilfred, 91
Think Big, Start Small, Move Fast, 38, 45
Third Side: Why We Fight and How We Can Stop, The, 143
Tolstoy, Leo, 116
Trading Places, 164

transistor revolution, 86
Trikaya Grey Advertising, 149
Trotsky, Leon, 141
Trust
  in an atmosphere of distrust, 145
  attitude, 144
  authenticity chips, 139
  authenticity, 139
  childhood, 151–5
  destroyed, 140–2
  distrust, 142
  emotions, 151–5
  empathy, 151–5
  faith in God and spirituality, 147
  feeling, 144
  Geeta's story and mission, 147
  generation, 138
  generosity, 147
  human unhappiness, 140
  relationship, 140, 144
  tribal societies, 137–8
  twist with, 68–9
Turkey, 49
Turmoil, 181–3
Tyco, scandals at, 109

ULPF, 53
UN ceasefire resolution, 168
Unilever Indonesia, 38, 45, 52–4
Union Baptist Church, 176

United Liberation Front for Assam (ULFA), 170
US presidential-type election, 1

Vaghul, N., 133–4
van Gogh, Vincent, 56, 59, 78, 81–2
Vasani, Bharat, 112
Venkateshwaran, A.P., 116–18
ventilation system of *punkawallahs*, 65
Venu, 103–6
Verdier, Madame Drinette, 174
Vibhishana, 124, 126–7
victimisation, feeling of, 15
Vishnu Saharanaam, 72
Vivekananda, Swami, 174–6

Wadi, Nusli, 181
Washington Post, 90
Watson, James, 166
Watson, John, 65
Watson, Thomas, 162
Western Union Company, 162
Westminster Cathedral, 50
What Sports Tells Us about Life, 177
Why Some People Thrive at the Limit, 91
Williams, Venus, 166
Willingdon Club, 55
work and family, 48–9
work-relationships balance, 14
WorldCom, scandals at, 109
Wright, Wilbur, 58

Yudhishtira, 67

Zimbardo, Philip, 19–20